NEW YORK'S FABULOUS LUXURY APARTMENTS

**With Original Floor Plans from
the Dakota, River House, Olympic Tower
and Other Great Buildings**

ANDREW ALPERN, AIA

With a Foreword by

Harmon H. Goldstone, FAIA
*Formerly Chairman,
New York City Landmarks Preservation Committee*

DOVER PUBLICATIONS, INC., NEW YORK

Published in Canada by General Publishing Company, Ltd., 30 Lesmill Road, Don Mills, Toronto, Ontario.
Published in the United Kingdom by Constable and Company, Ltd.

This Dover edition, first published in 1987, is an unabridged republication of *Apartments for the Affluent: A Historical Survey of Buildings in New York,* originally published by McGraw-Hill Book Company, New York, in 1975. A new photograph has been provided for page 3 and the corresponding credit has been altered on page 160.

Manufactured in the United States of America
Dover Publications, Inc., 31 East 2nd Street, Mineola, N.Y. 11501

Library of Congress Cataloging-in-Publication Data

Alpern, Andrew.
 New York's fabulous luxury apartments.

 Reprint. Originally published: Apartments for the affluent. New York: McGraw-Hill, c1975.
 Includes indexes.
 1. Apartment houses—New York (N.Y.)—Designs and plans.
2. Room layout (Dwellings)—New York (N.Y.)—Designs and plans.
3. Upper classes—New York (N.Y.)—Dwellings—Designs and plans.
4. New York (N.Y.)—Buildings, structures, etc.—Designs and plans.
I. Title
NA7860.A497   1987   728.3′1   86-24339
ISBN 0-486-25318-X

Thanks are owed to innumerable people who have helped with various aspects of the production of this book. Specific appreciation is due to:

- —The staff of the library and the print room of the New-York Historical Society for research assistance.
- —Charlotte LaRue of the Museum of the City of New York for help in locating photographs.
- —Harmon H. Goldstone for detailed assistance in connection with buildings designed by his father.
- —Henry and Chris Weiman, of Weiman & Lester, for their thoughtful care and professional skill in printing the photographs.
- —Paul Goldberger for specific help and general encouragement.
- —My parents, Grace and Dwight Alpern, for helpful criticism and encouragement.
- —Jeremy Robinson, without whom the book would never have been born.

These people helped with any merit this book may have; any errors are mine alone.

Andrew Alpern
New York

FOREWORD

For most New Yorkers, the word *apartment* is now so nearly synonymous with *home* — over 98 percent of Manhattan families currently reside in multiple dwellings — that it is hard to realize how shocking this idea once was. Edith Wharton, writing of that Age of Innocence, the 1870's, which she knew so well, describes how an old lady whose

> burden. . .of. . .flesh had long since made it impossible for her to go up and down stairs, and with characteristic independence. . .had. . .established herself (in flagrant violation of all the New York proprieties) on the ground floor of her house; so that, as you sat in her sitting-room. . .you caught. . .the unexpected vista of a bedroom. . .

> Her visitors were startled and fascinated by the foreignness of this arrangement, which recalled scenes in French fiction, and architectural incentives to immorality such as the simple American had never dreamed of. That was how women with lovers lived in the wicked old societies, in apartments with all the rooms on one floor, and all the indecent propinquities that their novels described.

In his historical survey of the apartment house in New York, Andrew Alpern traces the architectural evolution of *this arrangement* and the rapid social acceptance of *the indecent propinquities*. He does it through acute comments on chronologically arranged examples and through the inclusion of typical floor plans which convey more eloquently than pages of text the changes over a century in the manner of living of well-to-do New Yorkers.

Try to imagine yourself stepping out of the passenger elevator and then walking from the front door through each room of one of these apartments. You will discover, in early examples, how inconvenient the long, narrow halls must have been for entertaining, how scarce the bathrooms and closets, how miserable the servants' rooms, how far the cooked food had to be carried, and yet how ample the kitchens and pantries, how large the dining rooms, living rooms, libraries and foyers and, often, how graciously they were arranged. By the 1920's apartments have become truly palatial. Some of the duplexes and triplexes, with their roof gardens and terraces, have all the grandeur of great town houses. After the second World War, servants' rooms and dining rooms disappear, kitchens become tiny efficiency units, bedrooms shrink in number and in size, yet closets and bathrooms are lavishly plentiful (though the latter have lost the luxury of daylight), windows generally are much larger and the wall space in the living rooms, though limited, is usually planned for workable furniture arrangements.

Just as a century of social and economic change can be followed through the series of floor plans, so can the concurrent shifts in cityscape and architectural aesthetics be followed in the photographs that accompany them.

Residential development in American cities has typically gone through five successive stages: open land (either wild or farmed), closely spaced free-standing houses (the suburban pattern), row houses, row apartments and, finally, free-standing apartments. The succession, however, is rarely uniform or complete. Manhattan, for example, largely skipped the suburban pattern in which much of Queens and Staten Island is arrested today. Much of Brooklyn stopped with the row house. The Bronx jumped directly from open land to the row apartment. The free-standing apartment tower is a newcomer in all boroughs and its intrusion into the established texture of the city is causing considerable pain.

On aesthetic grounds alone there is understandable concern over what these towers are doing to the scale of their surroundings and the effect they are having on the visual quality of the street itself. A constant distance between the fronts of buildings facing one another across a street and their more or less uniform height have traditionally been among the strongest factors in establishing the character of a neighborhood. The free-standing residential tower has upset all this. While the more sensitive designs give hints of the possible evolution of a new sort of urban aesthetic, it is too early to prophesy the form it may take. But, however the problem is resolved as far as the cityscape is concerned, it can be incontestably stated now that the slender free-standing apartment house tower has forced the architect, for the first time, to consider his structure as a three-dimensional entity which must be designed with equal integrity from all sides and view points. Before its advent, the aesthetics of apartment house design typically consisted of two parts: the main façade and the rest of the building.

In regard to the façades, it must be kept in mind that the great era of luxury apartment building, 1870 to 1930, coincides almost exactly with the eclectic period in American architecture. The various renaissance and post-renaissance styles were particularly popular for residential work. What could be more natural than to transfer their application from houses to apartment houses? The difficulty was that styles which had evolved for three-, four- or five-story buildings now had to be adapted to structures which were eight, ten or fourteen stories high. The solution may be called design by inflation.

What had been a one-story base is now blown up to two, three or four stories. What had been a simple band or frieze under the crowning cornice now is enlarged to include one and sometimes two full stories. The left-over middle part of the building is treated more or less uniformly, though band-courses, balconies, pedimented windows and carved panels are introduced to break up what would otherwise have been a monotonous expanse. Cornices are either given an exaggerated projection in an attempt to hold down the sheer mass of these inflated structures, or else they are lowered one or two stories — with an enlarged *attic* or mansard roof above them — in order to reduce the building's apparent height. Vertical elements, too, are similarly inflated: pilasters, corner turrets, tiers of bay windows, wide banks of quoins or of rustication become multi-story affairs. Frequently the building mass itself is broken into by deep courtyards. These not only had the practical advantage of making more periphery available for windows but served to subdivide the huge volumes into manageable masses. Naturally the horizontal rhythms were more appropriate and, in the best examples, very imaginatively adapted to buildings designed in the classical tradition; vertical devices lent themselves more naturally to the few examples designed in the Gothic style. They also seem to have finally led a break with the pretense that a multi-story apartment house is really the same thing as a four- or five-story palazzo, only bigger. Schwartz and Gross' design of 1929 for 55 Central Park West, followed closely by two block-front, twin-tower structures by Chanin and Delamarre, are the earliest illustrations of an attempt to treat the apartment house as a thing in itself — as a unified whole from sidewalk to summit.

But returning for the moment to the eclectic architect whose work fills the bulk of this book: after he had designed his façade, how did he handle the rest of his building? With the very few exceptions that occupied an entire block, apartment houses were typically built shoulder to shoulder right up to the side lot lines. When the adjoining structures were lower, one or more party walls were left in plain view; the rear of these buildings was also exposed — if not from the street, then from apartments on the other side of the block. No matter how rich the materials and details of the façade might be, the rear and side walls were almost invariably faced with common red brick or inexpensive yellow brick. And then there were always such incongruous elements as stair and elevator bulkheads, air exhausts, chimneys and water tanks that stuck up above the roof. Having solved the problem of the main façade, the eclectic architect quite conveniently ignored these left-overs. He accepted as a convention that anything not part of the façade simply did not exist, just as the audience at a Japanese puppet show has trained itself not to see the men who manipulate the jointed dolls in plain view.

Insights into such matters as these and into much more await the browser of Andrew Alpern's innovative study. His book fills a gap in the appreciation of an important part of our cultural heritage. The importance of the luxury apartment house to the social and architectural history of New York City has been independently confirmed by the collective judgment of its Landmarks Preservation Commission. As of the end of 1974, no less than nine of the examples discussed in this book — The Chelsea, The Dakota, The Dorilton, The Ansonia, 131 East 66th Street, The Belnord, The Apthorp, Alwyn Court and 998 Fifth Avenue — had been officially designated as individual Landmarks because, in the words of the Landmarks law, they *represent or reflect elements of the city's cultural, social, economic, political and architectural history*. Four further examples — The Kenilworth, 44 West 77th Street, 35 West 9th Street and Butterfield House — are parts of designated Historic Districts which *have a special character or special historical or aesthetic interest or value* that make them distinctive sections of the city. Apartment dwelling is the only way of life that the vast majority of living residents of Manhattan has ever known. We owe it to ourselves to understand better how things became the way they are as well as where they may be heading.

HARMON H. GOLDSTONE, FAIA
Chairman, 1968-1973
New York City Landmarks Preservation Commission

CONTENTS

INTRODUCTION

The history of housing in New York is as much one of sociology as it is of architecture, especially where mass housing for the working classes is concerned. Many volumes have been written about tenement houses — touting them in the nineteenth century and condemning them in the twentieth. The pioneer efforts toward humane housing on a large scale by Ernest Flagg and I. N. Phelps Stokes have been well documented, as have the many large single and multiple residential developments of the 1930's and 40's which were designed to provide adequate accommodations for families of modest means.

Virtually ignored, however, have been individual apartment buildings designed for middle and upper income families. For a little more than a hundred years they have ranged from the merely functional to the grandly palatial. While some were planned and erected quickly for speculative purposes by financially motivated entrepreneurs, others were painstakingly designed by architects of wide reknown. The details of their planning and decoration reflect the tastes and life styles of New Yorkers over the past ten decades. As modes of living have evolved, so have the buildings which house them.

It may come as a surprise to most New Yorkers for whom apartment living has always been a way of life to find that apartments in the United States represent a relatively new housing concept. It has only been since 1869 that those who consider themselves above the laboring classes have been willing to make their homes under shared roofs. Prior to that time it would have been unthinkable for a family of even modest social aspirations to live in anything but a private dwelling, however humble such a house might be. Richard Morris Hunt, who was later to become the family architect for the Vanderbilt clan, changed these attitudes by importing the apartment house concept from Paris, where he had been the first American to study architecture at the Ecole des Beaux Arts. No doubt the impeccable social credentials of Rutherford Stuyvesant, who financed the venture, were also helpful in making the project a success.

The first apartments were available only on a rental basis under leases of negotiable duration. Then, around 1880, a cooperative-type arrangement in the form of a joint stock company was developed by the architectural/builder firm of Hubert, Pirsson and Company. Buildings erected under this system were known as Hubert Home Clubs. The apartments provided were generally duplexes (two floors), to reproduce as closely as possible the atmosphere of a private house. Elevator, door and hall men were employed and efforts were made to assure the privacy of each cooperator/tenant. The novelty of this sort of arrangement apparently wore off quickly, however, and the buildings erected after 1885 were again of the rental variety, cooperative apartments not reappearing until after World War I.

The earliest apartments contained most of the elements of a private house, though often assembled in a manner far from functional. The arrangement of the service spaces in particular was seldom designed to save the time or energy of those who regularly used them. But with household help cheap and easy to obtain, and wives who spent most of their time at home, most men were blissfully ignorant of these inadequacies. However, as more and more people abandoned the keeping of private houses in the city with the attendant necessity for small armies of servants to maintain them, builders found it expedient to attend more carefully to the planning of the new apartment houses in order to attract tenants. Nonetheless, the buildings that evolved would still have been regarded as inadequate by today's standards, although they served well enough for turn-of-the-century households.

Large windows and light rooms were not considered necessary or desirable, as contemporary tastes in decorating ran to heavy curtains and ponderous overdrapes. Dining rooms were often larger than living rooms (known then as parlors), which were reserved for company. The dining room, together with the reception hall or the library, was the real *living* room of the house. Bedrooms (chambers) were used primarily for sleeping and dressing and so were minimal in size. Closet space was often all but completely ignored, tenants being expected to provide their own storage space in the huge armoires then in vogue. More than one bathroom per family was uncommon and, of course, multiple telephone installations were unheard of. While servants were generally treated with respect, possibly for selfish reasons, their problems of personal hygiene were sometimes slighted, bathtubs for domestic help being considered a luxury. Most maids' rooms, however, were provided with sinks. Adjoining master bedrooms often were connected by a small sink closet, easing the strains on the bathroom facilities.

As the century progressed, the amenities offered increased. Central vacuum-cleaning systems, central refrigeration plants, wall safes, filtered water, telephone switchboard service, tradesmen's elevators and rear service entrances all became commonplace. Still, however, the long dark halls persisted along with thoughtlessly designed kitchens.

It was not until after the first World War that the off-the-foyer arrangement became widely used, supplanting the long-hall plan, which tied the apartment together with a long, narrow and often many-cornered corridor. The new mode of planning provided a reception room or entrance foyer from which one could go directly to the living and dining rooms, the kitchen, or the bedroom area, without having to traverse a long hall. Through the 1920's and into the early 30's, apartment layouts became more compact and functionally detailed. Façades became more refined and less susceptible to vindictive pigeons. Ways of lending individuality were used more widely: duplex and even triplex suites could be found, as well as duplexed units, where the bedrooms are on a floor above the entertaining rooms but not directly over them as they would be in a regular duplex. Interlocking apartments on alternate floors could yield higher ceilings in the living rooms than in the bedrooms. Sunken living rooms, one or two steps below the rest of the apartment, were a particular favorite during the thirties.

From the mid-thirties through World War II, very few really spacious apartments were built. Dining and servants' rooms became a rarity and most interior decorative elements disappeared, along with ceilings higher than 8'-6". However, by way of compensation, closet space grew, multiple bathrooms were provided, facilities were installed for telephones and for television antennas, and central air conditioning became standard.

The latest development has been the re-emergence of a few buildings for persons of unlimited means, which augment the run-of-the-mill (though expensive) apartments for the merely rich. Families of moderate income can no longer be housed in individual buildings but must content themselves with living in large government-subsidized developments.

Apartments in New York have ranged in size from one room with one bath to 54 rooms with 16 baths. The buildings containing these apartments have also varied widely in their dimensions. The narrowest house presently standing in Manhattan is on Bedford Street and is 9½ feet wide. This seems almost palatial compared to the one that stood on the northwest corner of 82nd Street and Lexington Avenue from 1882 until 1915. It was 102 feet long, but only 5 feet wide! It must certainly have been the narrowest building ever built and was undoubtedly the strangest apartment house known. In 1882, Hyman Sarner, a clothier, wanted to build an apartment house on a lot he owned on East 82nd Street. He lacked, however, the five-foot strip of land fronting on Lexington Avenue. He approached Joseph Richardson, who owned the strip, and offered him $1000 for the land. Richardson wanted $5000, which Sarner refused to pay. Undaunted, Sarner erected his house, with windows on the lot line. Apparently for spite, Richardson then erected his own house on the narrow strip. He lived in part of it until he died in 1897 at the age of 84, renting out the apartments in the rest of the building. The spiral staircase and the halls were too narrow for two people to pass, and the rooms were arranged railroad-car fashion, making it necessary to pass through one to get to the next. The furniture had to be specially built to fit, the dining table being only 18" wide, but somehow space was found for Richardson's coffin, which he kept in the house, having had it built from the wood of a tree he had specially selected in 1854!

1216 Lexington Avenue

While the Lexington Avenue building may have been the strangest apartment house, the St. Helene, on Broadway between 74th and 75th Streets, was probably the smallest. It contained only two suites, yet each included all the features that one would expect to find in a much larger building. It stood only for about 25 years, however, and was torn down to make way for Irwin Chanin's Hotel Beacon.

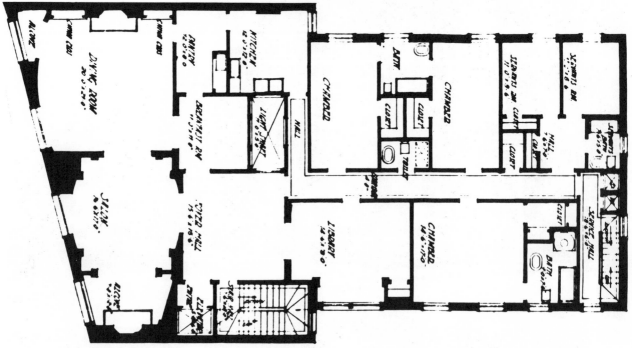

2128 Broadway

The smallest conventional apartment houses are the ones built on the standard 25' x 100' side street lot. This is the same size lot that might accommodate a one-family brownstone or a tenement house with four families per floor. When used for an apartment house, this size lot permits only two units to a floor and all but requires a courtyard in the middle, as shown below.

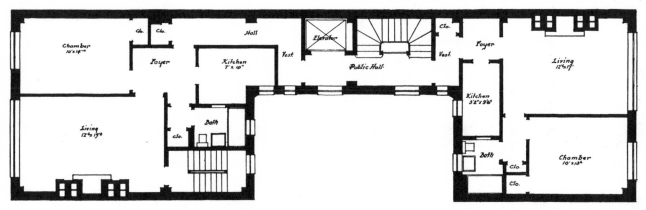

19 East 65th Street

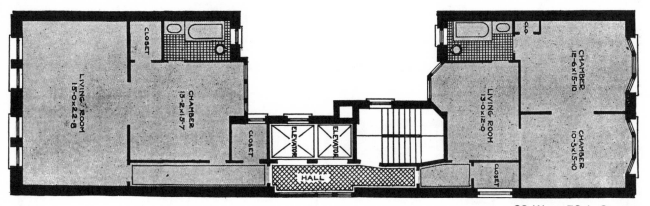

38 West 59th Street

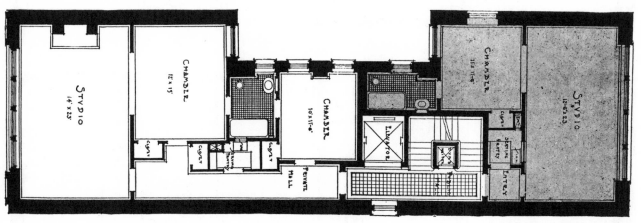

116 West 59th Street

The possibilities are more varied when the 25-foot lot is at the corner of a block. As these examples indicate, the building can be designed with one or two apartments to a floor, or with a duplex suite for each pair of floors.

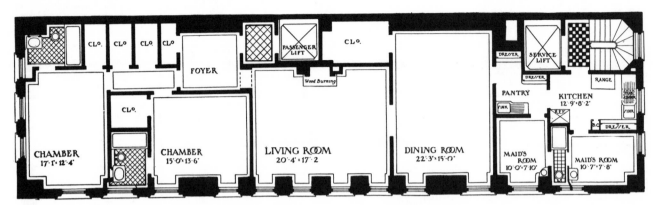

1 East 88th Street

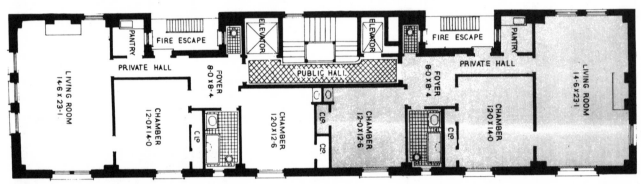

200 West 59th Street

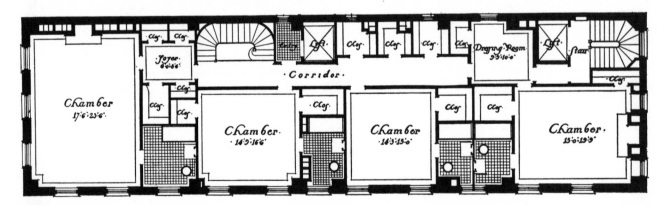

990 Fifth Avenue

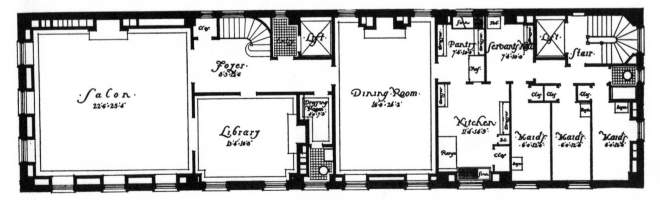

When an interior lot 40 or 50 feet wide is available, the most likely shape to be utilized is that of a T, as this arrangement enables at least three apartments to be placed on each floor. It should be noted that even in buildings as small as the two examples shown, each of which is nine stories high, there is a certain amount of unexpected amenity provided; the 38th Street building includes service entrances for the front apartments and two interior staircases while the one on 55th Street has two elevators plus a particularly well laid-out two-bedroom front apartment.

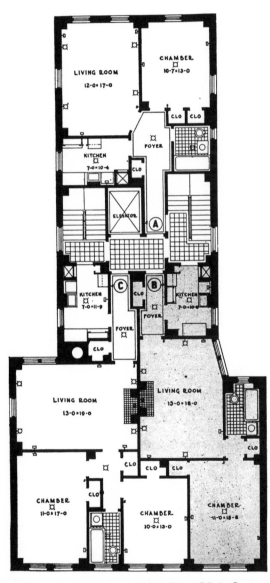

105 East 38th Street

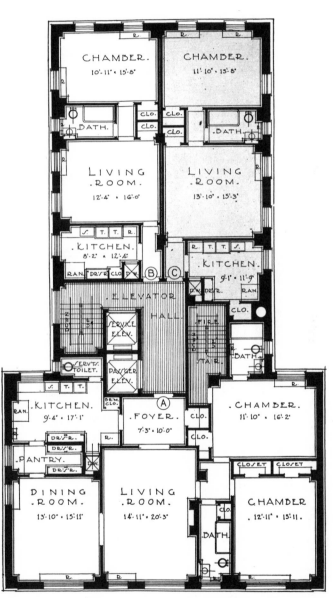

19 West 55th Street

With a building site larger than 50' x 100', the varieties of arrangement that can be devised are too numerous to summarize readily. At that point the dominant factor is no longer the size of the lot, but rather a combination of the market towards which the building is aimed, the number and size of apartments the builder wants to include, the investment to be made and the amount of mortgage money available, and of course the ingenuity of the architect. Although it is often unsung, the skill of the architect involved is frequently a deciding factor in the financial viability of a particular building. And the results of that skill can affect other architects and yield unanticipated benefits.

It has been said that imitation is the highest form of flattery, and architecture is not immune to this adage. New York has numerous cases, usually evident only by comparing floor plans. An interesting example is that of 760 and 660 Park Avenue. Both were ventures of Starrett Brothers, Inc. 760 Park was built first, designed by W.L.Rouse and L.A.Goldstone in 1924. It was evidently successful, as York & Sawyer, architects, designed 660 Park two years later with only minor modifications to the plan. 660 Park is particularly notable because, in addition to nine typical full-floor apartments, there is a spectacular maisonette consisting of the building's entire first, second and third floors. This apartment has its own address, 666 Park Avenue, and its own private entrance on 67th Street. A flight of broad marble steps leads to a foyer whose walls are carved Caen stone. On this level is a double-height living room 22' x 49', a double-height dining room and a double-height library, as well as a study, the kitchen, service pantries and the servants' hall. The second level includes separate men's and ladies' coat rooms and six servants' rooms. The third level contains the master suite (bedroom, sitting room, dressing room and bath) plus two other master bedrooms (each with its own bathroom) as well as a sewing room, extensive closet space, and five additional servants' rooms. The façade of 660 Park is divided with a balustrade and a continuous belt course that separates the maisonette from the rest of the building.

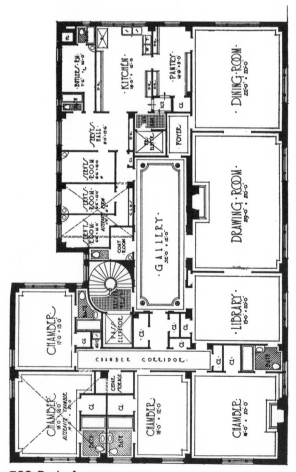

760 Park Avenue

660 Park Avenue

The lavishness of the interior of 666 Park Avenue approximates the ideal to which most builders of apartment houses have aspired, even up to the present day. Building lobbies range from tasteful to horrendous, and have generally reflected the prevailing decorating fashion. These examples are from buildings constructed between 1869 and 1908.

142 East 18th Street

135 Central Park West

41 Convent Avenue

44 West 77th Street

While entrance lobbies are at least semi-permanent, the interiors of the actual apartments are subject to the changing fancies of the tenants. Nonetheless, builders in the early part of this century lavished a considerable effort on the interior detailing of many of their apartments. The examples shown are from two West Side buildings.

135 Central Park West

135 Central Park West

380 Riverside Drive

380 Riverside Drive

Although the scope of this book is deliberately limited to individual apartment houses in Manhattan, certain other related buildings which also have contributed to the multiple residence stock of the city should be mentioned in passing.

One of the earliest attempts at a "multiple" dwelling for families of some social stature was The Spanish Row or House of Mansions on Fifth Avenue between 41st and 42nd Streets. Designed by Alexander Jackson Davis and built in 1855 by George Higgens, it was a series of individual town houses architecturally treated to appear as a single structure. Apparently the concept was not economically viable, because five years later the entire block was acquired by the Rutgers Female Institute.

Another early pseudo-apartment house was the Studio Building at 51-55 West 10th Street, designed in 1857 by Richard Morris Hunt for James Boorman Johnson. Although it contained living quarters, it was primarily intended to provide studios for artists, which it did until it was razed in 1954.

The buildings described on the following pages are arranged chronologically and are illustrated with contemporary views whenever possible. The plans shown are usually for typical floors and can be expected to be subject to minor variations within each building.

The Stuyvesant
142 East 18th Street

Architect: Richard Morris Hunt
Builder: Rutherford Stuyvesant
Built: 1869 (possibly a
              reconstruction of
              several older houses)
Razed: 1957

The Stuyvesant was the first building to house under one roof more than one family of the sort that aspires to high social status. Though lower class households had been accommodated together as early as 1833 in a tenement on Water Street, the quantity of the space and the quality of its occupants gives this building the distinction of being the first apartment house in New York. By present-day standards the layout was primitive: the kitchen, dining room, service entrance and dumbwaiter are all remote from each other; the inner hall is long and narrow and contains no less than five right-angle turns; two of the bedrooms are at the opposite end of the apartment from the lone bathroom; the closet space is inadequate; and no elevator was provided. Nonetheless **The Stuyvesant** represented a beginning and as such it is significant.

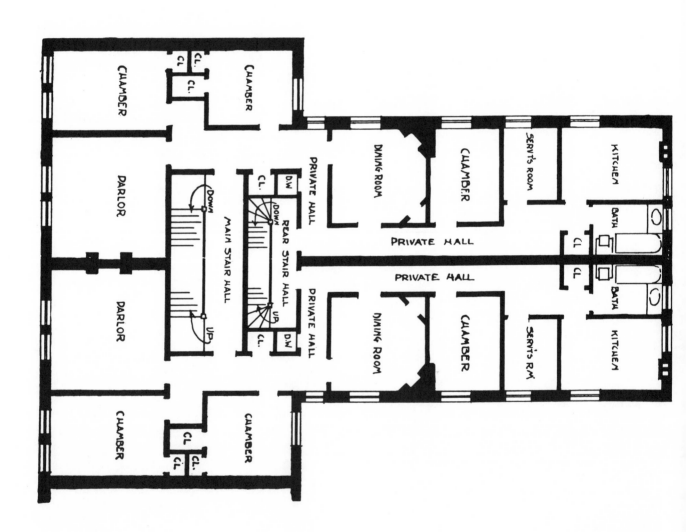

121 Madison Avenue

Architect:	Hubert, Pirsson and Company
Builder:	Hubert, Pirsson and Company
	Grosvenor P. Lowry
Built:	1883
Remodelled:	1940
Architect:	Mayers, Murray and Phillip
Builder:	Skinner, Cook and Babcock

This building, one of the original Hubert Home Clubs, consisted of five duplex apartments on each two floors, each sold on a cooperative basis. These were large and surprisingly compact in layout, as can be seen from the original plans, shown below. As might be expected for the period, when backyard privies were still in use in some parts of the city, each apartment had but one bathroom for as many as four bedrooms, and no facilities other than a water closet for the servants. In 1940 the building's interior was gutted, new elevators and stairs installed and numerous 2- and 3-room suites created. At the same time, the exterior was stripped of its cornice, its little balconies and almost all of its ornamentation. Almost nothing is left to even hint at the building's former distinguished status.

 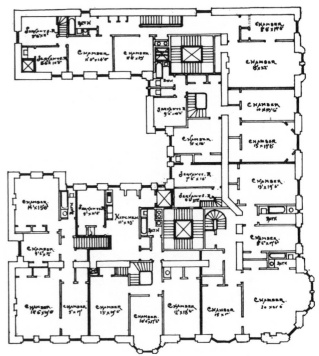

The Central Park Apartments
7th Avenue, 58th to 59th Streets

Architect:	**Hubert, Pirsson and Company**
Builder:	**Juan de Navarro**
Built:	**1883**
Razed:	**1927**

Commonly referred to as **The Spanish Flats**, this 8-building complex was planned as a cooperative venture. However, the original scheme fell through and the project was completed as a conventional rental structure by J. Jennings McComb, the original mortgagee, at a cost of over $4 million. Each building contained 13 apartments, of which 3 were double size. Additional maids' rooms and storage space was provided in the basement for the larger suites. Of particular interest was the provision for deliveries. A vehicular tunnel was constructed leading from an adjacent private street directly to the basements. Goods could thus be handled under cover and off the street. The buildings were especially notable for the lavishness of their interior decoration, yet all that remains today is the name of the original builder, now gracing a nearby hotel.

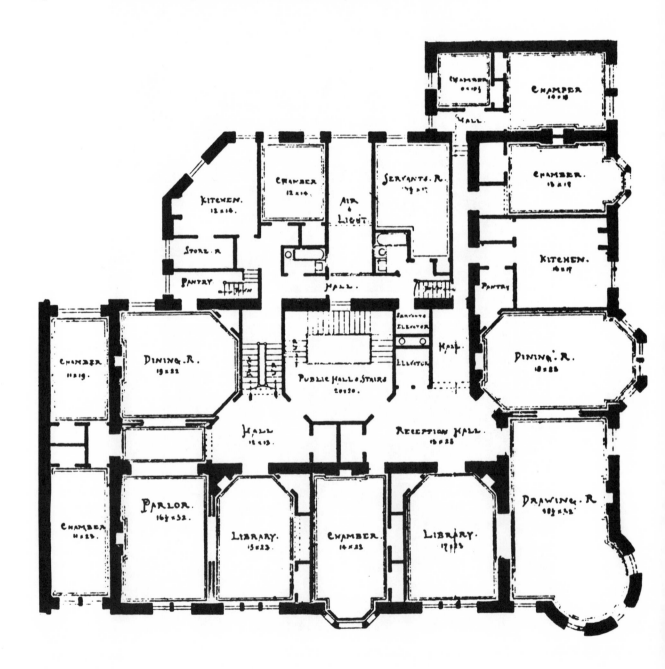

The Chelsea
222 West 23rd Street

Architect:	Hubert, Pirsson and Company
Builder:	Hubert, Pirsson and Company
Built:	1883
Converted to a hotel:	1905

The Chelsea, distinctive for its ornamental cast iron balconies, was an early apartment house operated primarily as a cooperative. Of the 90 original apartments, which ranged in size from 3 to 9 rooms, 30 were rented on a lease basis, as were the ground floor stores. Also included on the ground floor was a large restaurant together with several private dining rooms, as most of the apartments lacked full kitchen facilities. By 1905 the building's location was no longer fashionable, resulting in its conversion to a hotel. Curiously, as a gracious Edwardian hostelry, it has regained status in recent years. The present layout as a hotel, a typical floor of which is shown below, consists of numerous single rooms and 1-bedroom suites. The top floor has several larger units duplexed to studios on the roof.

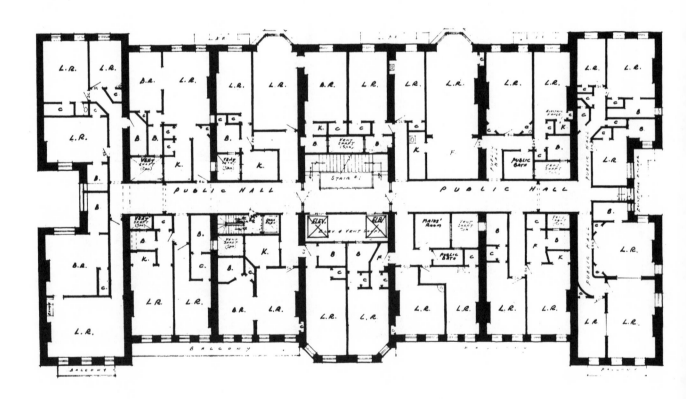

The Dakota
1 West 72nd Street

Architect: Henry Janeway Hardenbergh
Builder: Edward Severin Clark
Built: 1884
Converted to co-op: 1961

Not the first, but certainly the most famous, **The Dakota** is the Dowager Queen Mother of apartment houses. It was built in a style that can best be described as Brewery Gothic Eclectic, or as one tenant put it, Middle-European Post Office. As the forerunner of latter day luxury apartment buildings, it originally contained an impressive array of service spaces, including a large wine cellar, extensive kitchens, and a baronial dining hall for private parties, all of which have since been converted to additional apartments. The adjacent great lawn was later made over into tennis courts, which in turn were removed for a newer apartment tower. Master Mason John Banta took four years to complete **The Dakota**, building it in a manner intended to last for centuries. If the economics of the situation permit, it doubtless will.

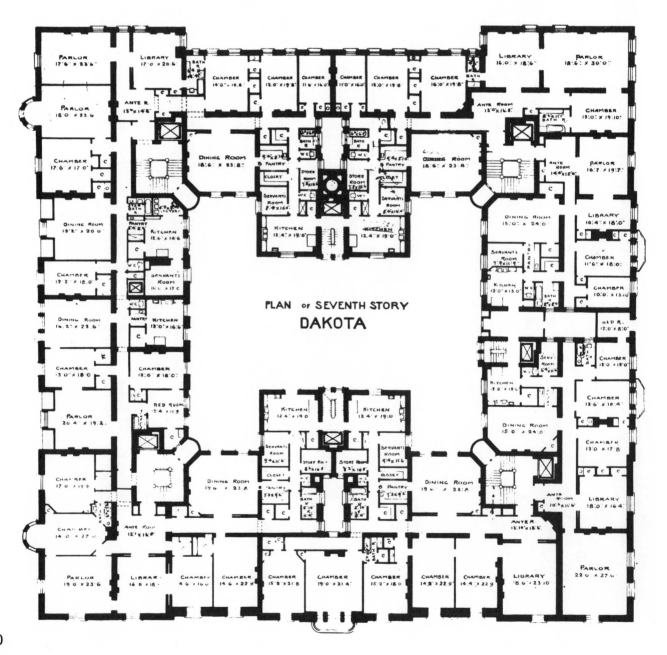

PLAN of SEVENTH STORY
DAKOTA

21

The Osborne
205 West 57th Street

Architect:	James E. Ware
Builder:	Thomas Osborne
	John Taylor
Built:	1885
Addition:	1910
Architect:	Taylor and Levi
Builder:	Taylor, Freeman and Ely

Due to its proximity to Carnegie Hall and its solid, sound-resistive construction, **The Osborne** has long housed musicians and others in the arts in a heavily rusticated Renaissance palazzo style. The building was begun by Thomas Osborne, a stone contractor, and was completed by John Taylor, a hotel operator, after Osborne went bankrupt. The interiors are ponderously lavish, with extensive mahogany woodwork, bronze mantels, crystal chandeliers and elaborate parquet flooring. The entrance lobby, ornately decorated in marble and stone, includes mosaic-encrusted walls, bronze bas-relief sculpture panels and two sweeping staircases. The front section of the building contains the major rooms of each apartment, with 15-foot ceilings. The service and sleeping rooms in the back have 8-foot ceilings providing semi-duplex apartments. In 1910 a narrow extension was placed on the building (so skillfully that it is virtually indistinguishable from the original building) containing additional bedrooms for the extreme westerly apartments. The plan shown below is from that period. In more recent years many of the apartments have been subdivided, the entrance portico removed and the first floor converted to stores. One of them, The Grenoble Market, is a remnant of a contemporary hotel of that name which formerly stood across the street from **The Osborne**.

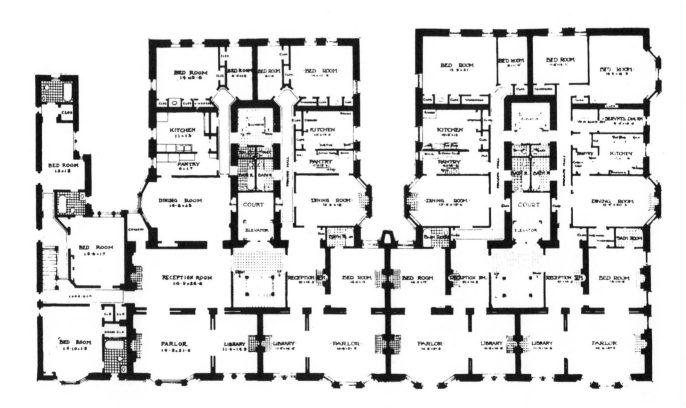

23

New Century Apartments
401 West End Avenue

Architect: William B. Franke
Builder: William B. Franke
Built: 1900
Remodelled: 1935
Architect: J.M.Berlinger
Builder: Excelsior Savings Bank

This building is distinctive both in plan and in outward appearance. The façade is a curious combination of styles. The entrance porch is Roman and the balconies and quoins Italian renaissance. The corners are rounded in the French manner, while the anthemia above the cornice line are pure Greek. The original floor plan, illustrated, was unusual for a middle-class apartment house in that it provided separate freight and service elevator entrances to each apartment as well as additional master bath facilities. The circulation pattern for each apartment was more straight-forward than most, with an entrance hall, off of which opened the major rooms, and a single straight inner hall leading to the bedrooms. A small garage for the residents' automobiles was provided adjacent to the building on 79th Street. In 1942 this two-story appendage was converted for use as a synagogue, in which capacity it presently serves. Unhappily, the original 10- and 11-room apartments have been cut into smaller units, seven to a floor, and the façade mutilated through the removal of the cornice as well as the entrance porch.

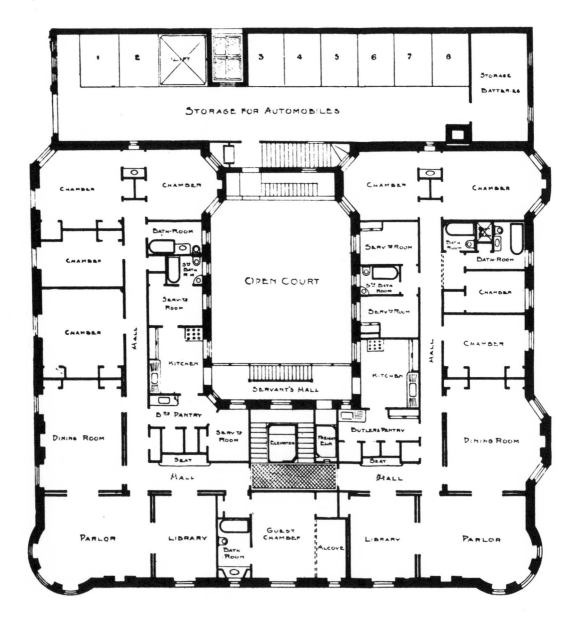

Graham Court
1923-1937 Seventh Avenue

Architect: Clinton and Russell
Builder: The Astor Family
Built: 1901

Graham Court, the prototype for the Apthorp built in 1908 on West 79th Street, was designed a few years earlier by the same architects. It is smaller than its more famous relative and more modest in its use of materials and ornamentation, but it does boast a handsome two-story Palladian entrance passageway to the interior court. The plan is similar to that of the Apthorp, the circulation being divided among four passenger elevators, each of which serves three apartments. The suites themselves generally contain spacious front rooms, usually including a very large foyer or reception room. The bedrooms, however, are quite small, and the apartments, with the exception of the corner units, have awkward circulation patterns and wholly inadequate closet space.

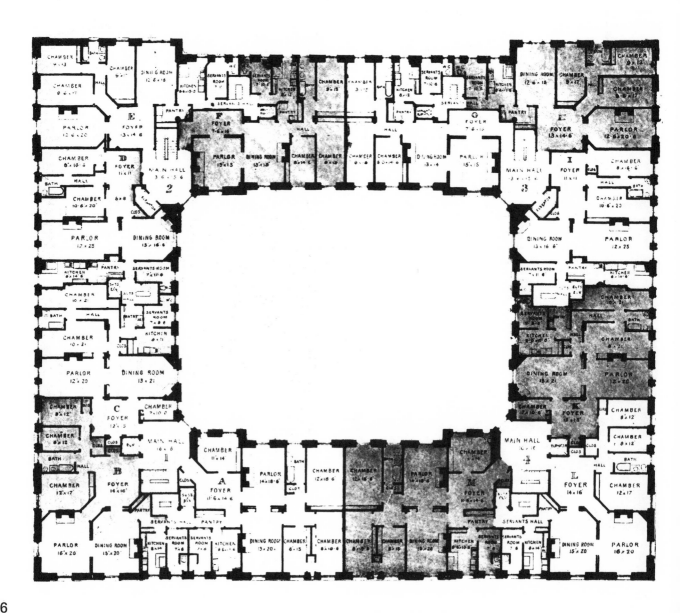

The Dorilton
171 West 71st Street

Architect: Janes and Leo
Builder: Hamilton W. Weed
Built: 1902

When **The Dorilton** was completed, The Architectural Record, a journal not generally given to strong language, called it *an architectural aberration* and said that *the sight of it makes strong men swear and weak women shrink affrighted.* After more than seventy years of enduring New York's polluted air, its appearance has mellowed but its overblown Second Empire pretensions remain, in spite of the conversion of much of the ground floor to stores. Still visible are the well-muscled stone men surveying a once elegant West Side from their perch four stories above Broadway. Visible too are the outsized cannon balls and the playful cherubs at the grandiose main entrance.

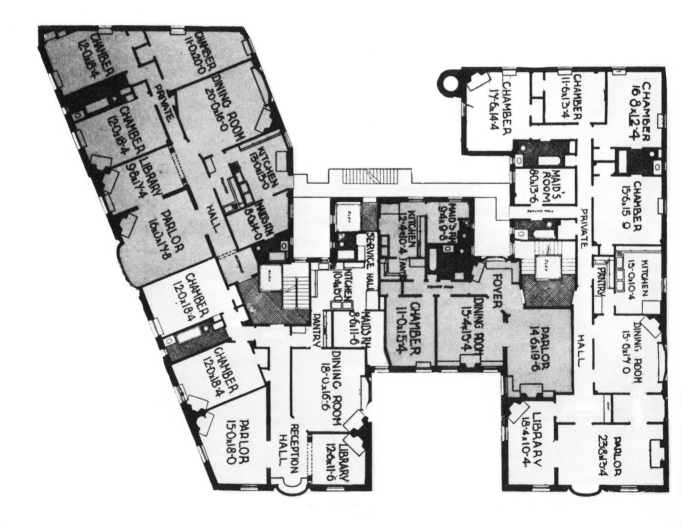

The Ansonia
2107 Broadway

Architect: Graves and Duboy
Builder: W. E. D. Stokes
Built: 1902

The Ansonia, strictly speaking an apartment-hotel, is an oversized version of a French resort hotel of the nineteenth century. Its fanciful turrets, balconies and carvings have helped earn for it the status of a registered historic landmark. The original floor plan included some of the most distinctive rooms ever assembled in one building. One apartment had an ellipsoidal living room, a similar dining room and a bedroom with one end shaped like the apse of a church. Another had a circular parlor, and an oval reception hall with a semi-circular sculpture niche. While some of these rooms remain, the apartments that contained them have been brutally cut up.

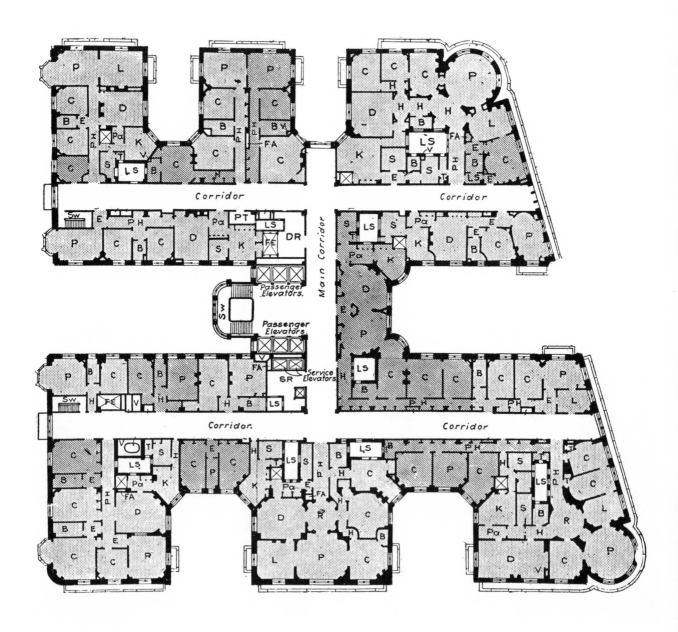

667 Madison Avenue

Architect:	Horgan and Slattery
Builder:	Frederick Haberman
Built:	1902
Converted:	1924
Architect:	Christian Francis Rosborg
	Montague Flagg
Builder:	Fred Haberman Trust
	Sylvester Haberman, Trustee

Despite its conversion to a commercial structure, this building retains traces of its former elegance. The limestone facing and the second-story carved figures remain, although the cornice and the porte-cochere are gone. Some of the rooms still show the original parquet flooring and high ceilings, but not the classically carved plasterwork moldings. It is only from the old floor plan, shown below, that we can really see what the original apartments were like. Two to a floor, the most striking feature is the parlor/library, 20 feet by 48 feet. Also to be noted are the two pantries as well as the additional fixtures in the master bathrooms. In 1920 plans were drawn for conversion to a hotel, but this scheme was never realized. Then, four years later, the same architects renovated the structure to provide a small hospital on the top three floors with doctors' offices in the remainder of the building. In later years the hospital was reconverted to apartments and subsequently some of those apartments were changed into offices. It is in this hybrid state that **667 Madison** presently exists.

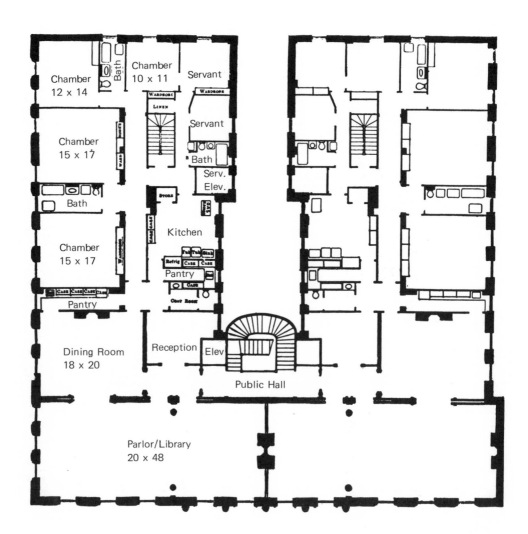

33

The Orienta
302 West 79th Street

Architect: Schneider and Herter
Builder: Abraham Morganroth
Built: 1904

The Orienta is an excellent example of an early symmetrical H-plan layout. The two front apartments are mirror images of each other, containing 7 rooms each. False fireplaces were included, along with both electric and gas lighting fixtures. The two rear apartments are almost identical, one having a maid's room and the other not. The advantage of a compact public hall on each floor unfortunately necessitated outside fire escapes, as only one interior stair was provided. Also unfortunate were the long entrance halls provided in the front units. The loss of one advantage of its location touted in a 1910 advertisement for the building is particularly to be lamented: *It is high, has perfect drainage and, because of its proximity to the Hudson, Riverside Drive and Central Park, enjoys the purest air.* Also lost is the spaciousness of the front apartments, which were subdivided in 1960.

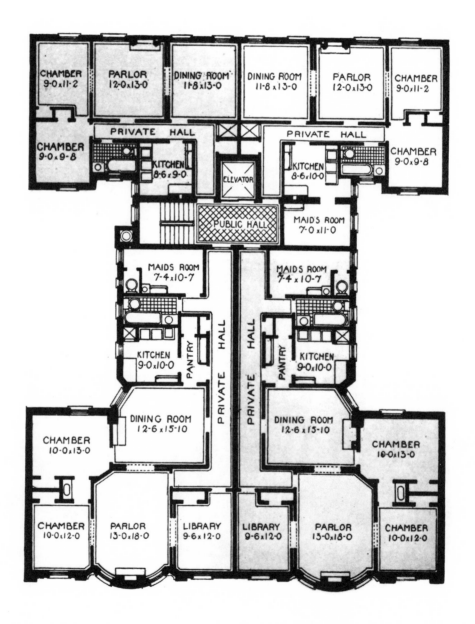

The Chatsworth
346 West 72nd Street

Architect:	John E. Scharsmith
Builder:	George F. Johnson, Jr.
	Aleck Kahn
Built:	1904

The Chatsworth is really two separate buildings with a common ground floor and entrance. The apartments on the upper floors range from a 1-bedroom unit (with a maid's room!) to one with 15 rooms, 4½ baths and a laundry. Commanding a fine view of the Hudson and the Palisades, the building offered its residents a broad variety of services and special accommodations including a cafe, a billiard room, a barber shop, a hair-dressing parlor, and valet and tailoring services. A sun parlor was provided which ran across the entire top floor, and electric bus service was maintained along 72nd Street from Central Park West to the building. Needless to say, these amenities have disappeared long since. In 1906 the builders of **The Chatsworth** erected an annex immediately adjacent to the building containing 8 apartments, each with 11 rooms and 4 baths. These have since been subdivided into smaller units.

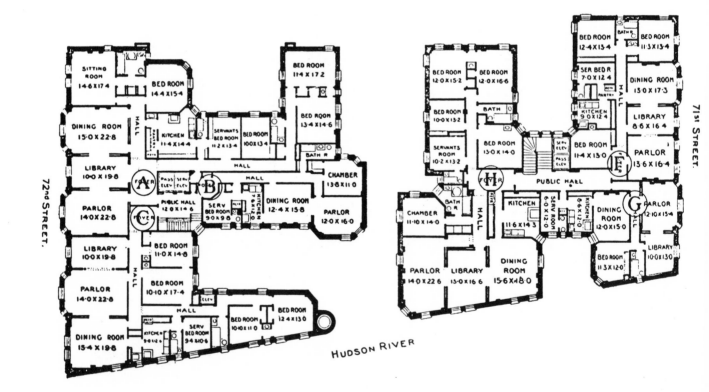

37

The Langham
135 Central Park West

Architect:	Clinton and Russell
Builder:	Boehm and Coon
Built:	1905
Remodelled:	1958-1960
Architect:	Wechsler and Schimenti
Builder:	Langham Mansions Company

The Langham, occupying the entire blockfront from 73rd to 74th Streets, originally contained only four apartments to a floor as shown on the plan below, most of which have since been divided into smaller units. The decorative moldings used in each apartment varied from floor to floor, and were exceptionally lavish, utilizing several different *period* styles. The entrance lobby was ornately decorated with bronze, marble, carved Caen stone and crystal chandeliers. Unused now for many years, there was originally an arcaded carriage driveway with access from 73rd Street. Among the amenities once provided were a direct-to-each-apartment mail conveyor system, a central refrigeration plant in lieu of ice-boxes, and built-in vacuum cleaning system connections and wall safes in each apartment. The original rents ranged upward from $4,500 per year.

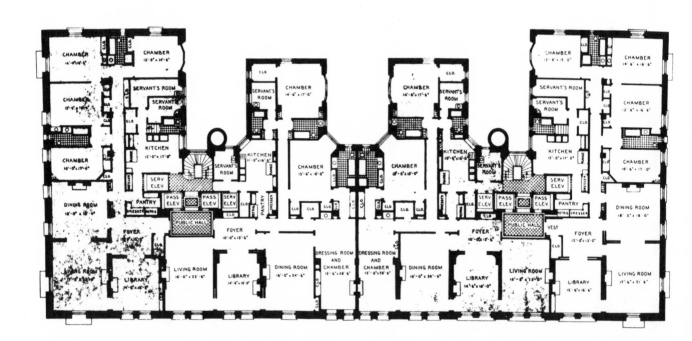

The Manhassett
301 West 108th Street
300 West 109th Street

Architect: Janes and Leo
Builder: Walter Reid and Company
Built: 1904

Anticipation of the extension of the subway system to upper Broadway doubtless influenced the builders to erect this apartment house, which originally contained suites of 2- to 4-bedrooms, many of which have since been subdivided. The apartments included libraries as well as such odd little rooms as a *lounging hall* and a *saloon.* Typical for its time was the inclusion of a sink-in-a-closet adjacent to some of the bedrooms as well as the exclusion of a bathtub in any of the servants' bathrooms. A broad range of accommodations was offered, with the apartments with the best exposure also having the largest rooms. Nonetheless, each of the units was of the *long hall* variety with rooms strung out along a dark and twisting corridor.

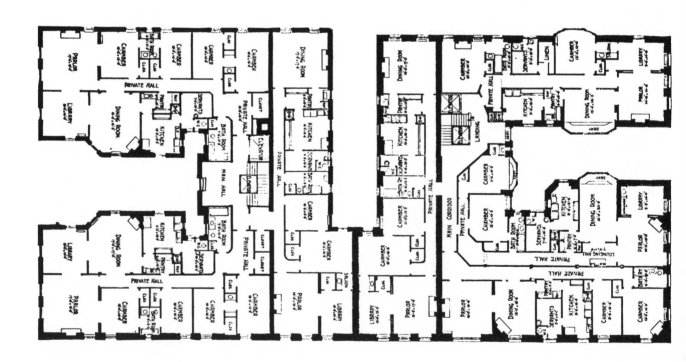

The Hendrik Hudson
380 Riverside Drive

Architect:	William L. Rouse
Builder:	Johnson-Kahn Company
Built:	1907

This building has had a curious three-part career. It began as a luxurious Tuscan-villa-style residence of large gracious apartments. A billiard room, a cafe and a barber shop were provided as well as a roof garden overlooking the Hudson. After World War II the apartments were broken up for single-room occupancy. This arrangement, which was used by a succession of owners to wring from the building the maximum financial return possible, attracted a tenancy that, together with the owners' minimal maintenance, caused the building's rapid deterioration. Public outrage, provoked by a newspaper article reporting the grusome death of a young boy in the building, who was crushed by one of the elevators, precipitated the re-conversion of the interior to small apartments. An independent addition on Broadway, built shortly after **The Hendrik Hudson**, has been similarly converted.

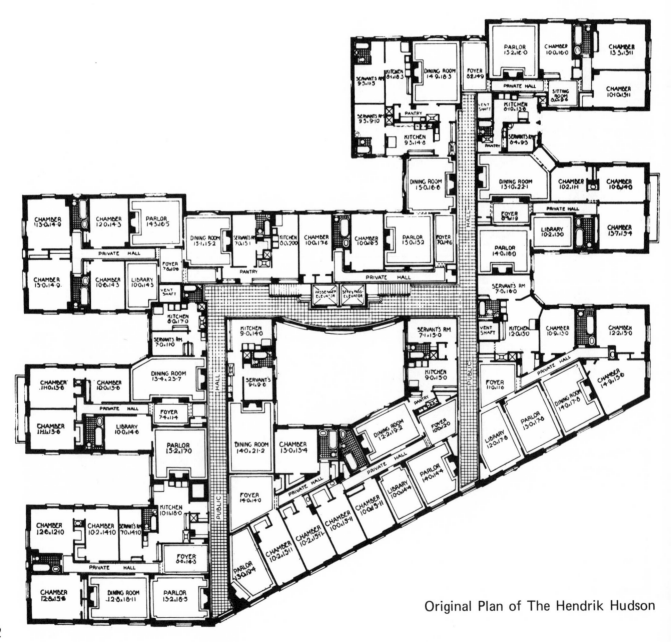

Original Plan of The Hendrik Hudson

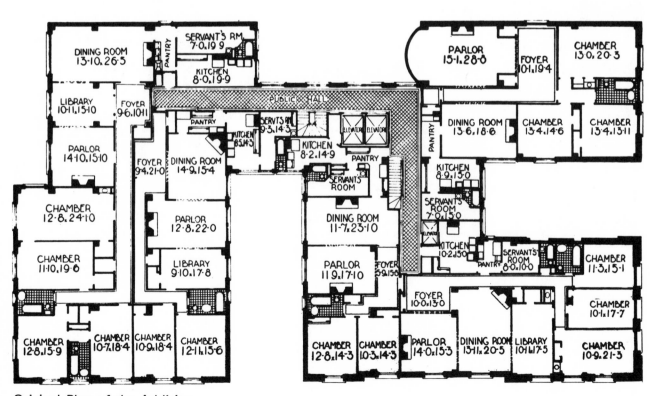

Original Plan of the Addition

131 East 66th Street

Architect:	Charles A. Platt
Builder:	William J. Taylor
Built:	1907, co-op

This building, originally containing the town apartment of its architect, is comprised primarily of duplex units, each designed around a spacious double-height living room. Costing $890,000 to construct, the building was soon followed by a sister structure at 130 East 67th Street designed by the same architect. That one, however, contains no high studios, but rather is a strange combination of very large duplexes and very small flats. Shown below is a comparison of similar rooms in **131 East 66th Street.** The one on the right dates from about 1912 and was part of the building's architect's own suite. The other dates from the present.

The Prasada
50 Central Park West

Architect: Charles W. Romeyn
                        Henry R. Wynne
Builder: Franklin and Samuel Haines
Built: 1907

The Prasada is a heavy-handed interpretation of the French Second Empire style. Its exterior detailing is crude, but its interiors are lavishly decorated, at least by today's standards. Each floor originally contained three apartments—two with 4 bedrooms and one with 3. The rooms are spacious but, typically for the period, the hallways are long and dark, and the closet space is minimal. In 1919 the original mansard roof was removed and the top floor correspondingly enlarged. The ground floor contains a pleasant extra-height entrance loggia, off of which open two suites, each containing a circular foyer. These have been converted to professional use and, in addition, some of the apartments on the upper floors have been divided into smaller units.

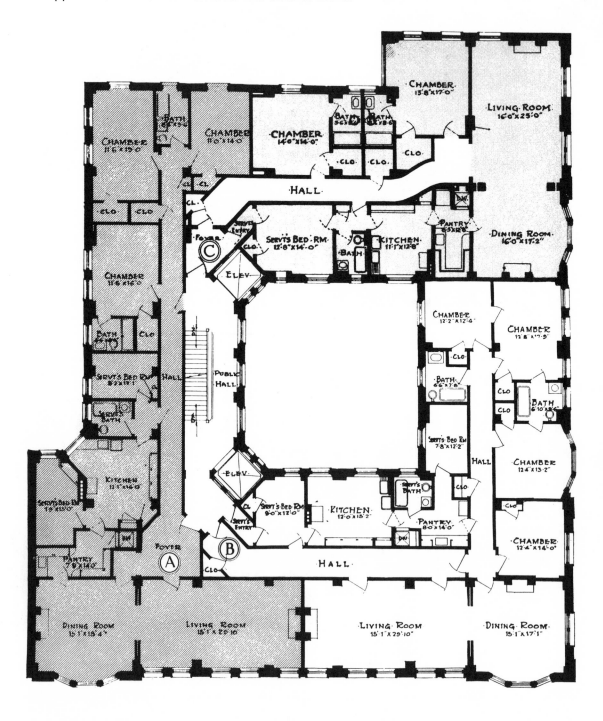

The Kenilworth
151 Central Park West

Architect: Townsend, Steinle and Haskell
Builder: Lenox Realty Company
Built: 1908
Converted to co-op: 1957

The Kenilworth has three apartments on each floor, two of which are of a modified long-hall variety. While not exceptional in their planning or appointments, these suites have been kept surprisingly intact, considering their age. Minor interior alterations have been wrought over the years, but the exterior of the building has hardly changed from the architect's original intentions. The French Second Empire styling has been retained and even the iron railinged moat is still to be seen.

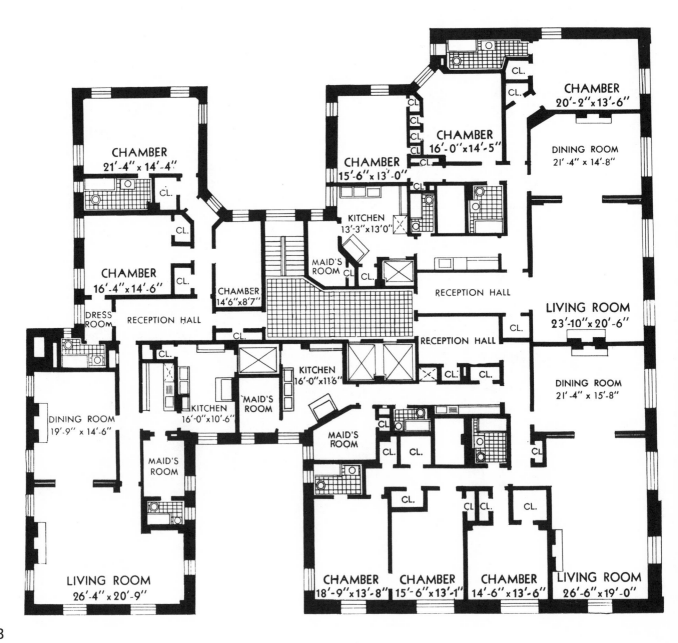

The Belnord
225 West 86th Street

Architect:	H. Hobart Weekes
Builder:	Belnord Realty Company
Built:	1908

The Belnord occupies a full city block and surrounds an interior courtyard of exceptionally ample proportion. From this landscaped garden court, access is gained to the six separate passenger elevator lobbies. These in turn lead to the upper floors, of which there are two distinct types. The majority consist of 16 suites, variously containing from 2 to 4 bedrooms. Some suites include a run-on parlor/library/dining room that spans the 50 feet from the interior court to the avenue. Four of the upper floors provide apartments with double-sized living and dining rooms. Ornamental details throughout the building lend a touch of elegance, although the structure lacks the grace and refinement of the Apthorp, shown on the next page, which was built at the same time, but by a different architect.

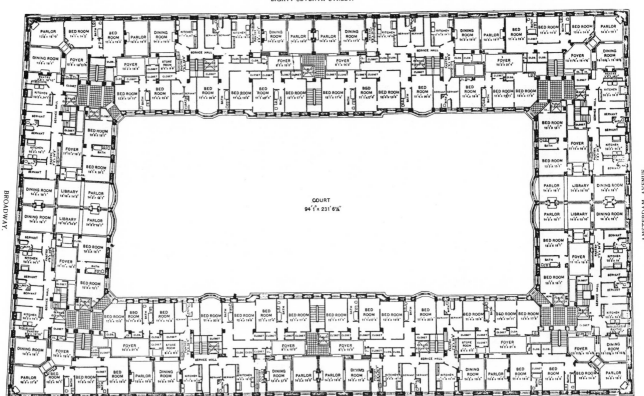

50

The Apthorp
2207 Broadway
390 West End Avenue

Architect: Clinton and Russell
Builder: John Downey for the Astor family
Built: 1908

Not nearly as large as its stylistic cousin, The Belnord, shown on the previous page, **The Apthorp** originally contained ten apartments to a floor, opening off four elevator halls. During the thirties and forties many of these were cut into smaller units to accommodate changing patterns of urban living. The apartments are particularly well detailed, with each of the original suites containing a room-sized foyer with a mosaic tile floor. There are glass-panelled French doors throughout, and many of the rooms are ringed with Wedgwood-esque friezes. The exterior of the building, facing both the street and the fountained court, is of limestone, beautifully carved and rusticated. The façades facing the avenues are superb compositions embodying bas relief sculptures, fully carved figures, numerous cherubs, and delicate wrought ironwork.

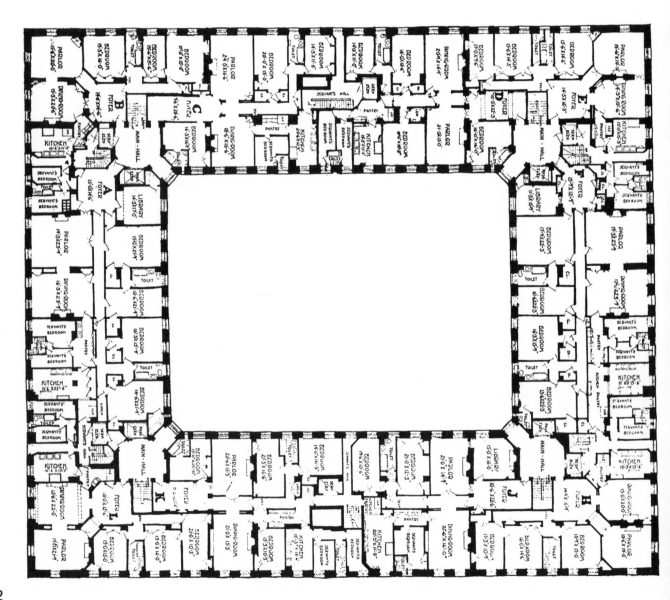

Alwyn Court
180 West 58th Street

Architect:	Harde and Short
Builder:	Hedden Construction Company
Built:	1908
Remodelled:	1938
Architect:	Louis S. Weeks
Builder:	Edgar Ellinger

Alwyn Court was named after Alwyn Ball Jr., a director of the company that built it. It originally housed 22 families in an approximation of French Renaissance splendor. The apartments, exceptionally spacious even for pre-World War I buildings, were decorated with carved Caen stone, marble and fine wood panelling. The dressing rooms had storage closets fitted with plate glass shelves and multiple full-length mirrors. A virtually identical structure was designed by the same architect and built at the same time by Charles F. Rogers at Madison Avenue and 66th Street. By 1938, however, the Depression had so dried-up the market for grandiose living accommodations that the apartments of **Alwyn Court** were going begging. Accordingly, armed with $200,000 from the Drydock Savings Bank, Edgar Ellinger gutted the building, leaving only the exterior walls and the floor beams, and rebuilt it to provide 75 apartments of 3, 4 and 5 rooms. It is in this state that it survives today.

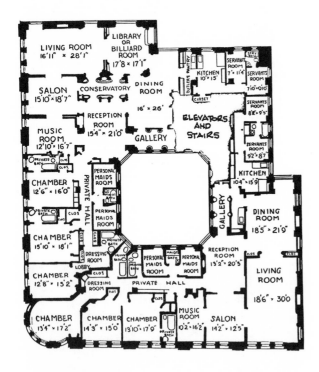

Original Plan

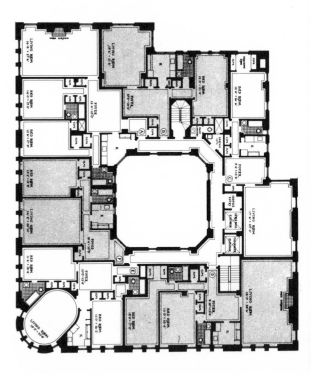

Remodelled Plan

The Turin
333 Central Park West

Architect: Albert Joseph Bodker
Builder: Sturtyvant Realty Company
Built: 1909

Strong lines and good proportion distinguish **333** from its newer neighbors. Its four tower-like sections contain six large apartments per floor, all of the *long hall* variety. In each case the entrance to the suite is at one end of a narrow corridor leading to the living and dining rooms. The only advantage to be gained from this rather dismal arrangement is that the sleeping rooms are well removed from the entertaining spaces, which in most of the apartments include an additional windowed reception room. The building originally boasted open cage-work elevator shafts with elaborately grilled cabs, but these, alas, have long since been replaced.

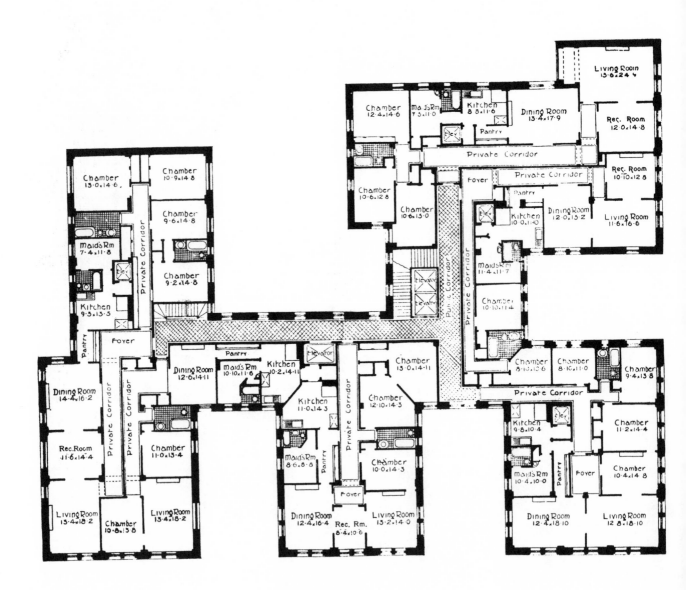

509 Cathedral Parkway

Architect:	Schwartz and Gross
Builder:	Carlyle Realty Company
Built:	1909
Remodelled:	1934
Architect:	Voorhees, Gmelin and Walker
Builder:	Emigrant Industrial Savings Bank

The original layout of this inverted-U shaped building consisted of four apartments per floor, all of the *long hall* variety. They were somewhat different from most, however, in that the principal rooms (living room, dining room, library) were near the entrance, while the bedrooms were at the end of the hall, facing the street. By 1934 these apartments were able to yield an average rental of only a little more than $9 per room per month. A total remodelling of the interior of the building was required to return it to a reasonable income-producing structure. New units were created providing a variety of apartment sizes more in keeping with newer styles of living. Room configurations and arrangements were improved and new kitchen and bathroom fixtures provided.

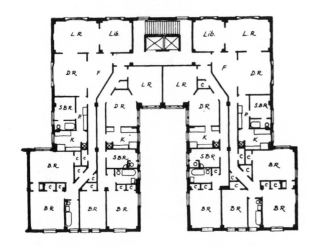

Original Plan

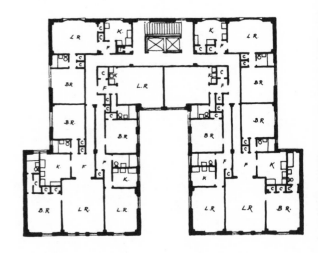

Remodelled Plan

44 West 77th Street

Architect: Harde and Short
Builder: Walter Russell Bond and Realty Company
Built: 1909, co-op
Converted to rental
Reconverted to co-op: 1970

Unfortunately, in 1944, much of the delightful gingerbread which originally adorned the façade of this building was removed, victim of the corrosive New York City air which had disintegrated the stonework's mortar. The interior, however, has been left intact, complete with the gothic-style groin-vaulted lobby, the stone foyers, and the elaborately panelled dining rooms. Of particular interest are the extra-height studios in most of the apartments. The largest is on the top floor and is 25 feet by 44 feet with an 18-foot ceiling.

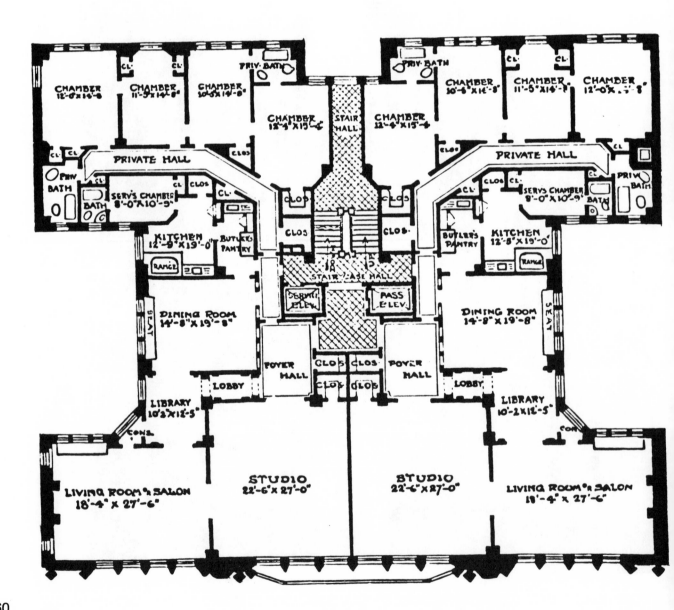

The Lucania
235 West 71st Street

Architect: Gaetano Ajello
Builder: Anthony Campagna
Built: 1910

An early example of an H-plan layout, this building displays an asymmetrical arrangement of 3- to 6-room suites, which gives an economic advantage to the rental agent. The original rents ranged from $900 to $2,000 per year. There is only one interior stair, necessitating outside fire escapes, which are a strange contrast to the luxury features originally provided including two elevators, continuously circulating hot water and filters between the city water supply and the faucet outlets. It is interesting to note the comment on the availability of servants in 1910 inherent in the provision for sleep-in maids in two of the four apartments on each floor as well as the formal dining rooms in three of them.

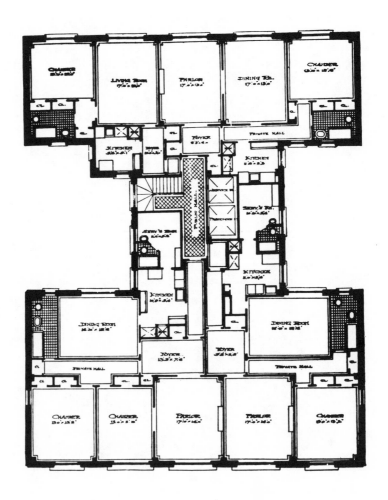

Colosseum
435 Riverside Drive

Architect:	Schwartz and Gross
Builder:	Dr. Charles V. Paterno
Built:	1910

A curiously curved structure, this building is the sister to one across the street by the same builder. Paterno, a medical doctor by training, took over the family construction business with his younger brother Joseph upon his father's unexpected death, never returning to the practice of medicine. His own fantasy castle/home on Washington Heights stood until 1938. **Colosseum** originally contained 8- and 12-room simplex apartments and three 10-room duplexes. Needless to say, these units have long since been subdivided, but the building retains much of its original elegance and grace, and of course the superb views of Riverside Park and the Hudson.

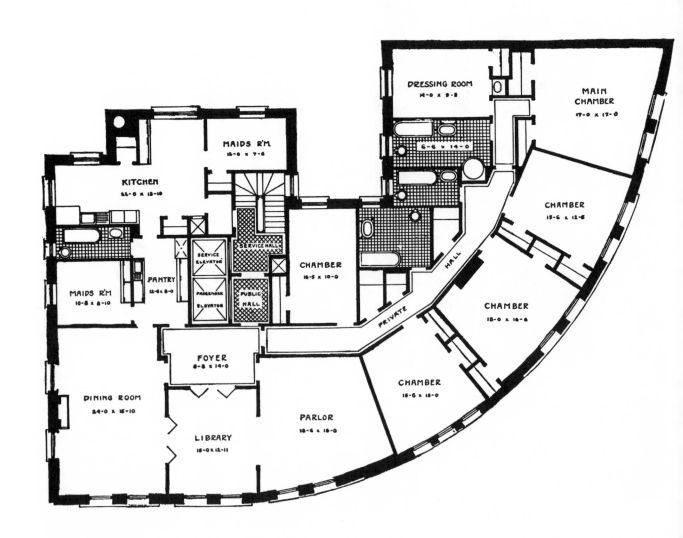

The Dorset
150 West 79th Street

Architect:	**Schwartz and Gross**
Builder:	**Vadrick Realty Company**
Built:	**1910**
Remodelled:	**1937**
Architect:	**Boak and Paris**

While most H-plan buildings had four apartments per floor, this one originally had but two. Most of the units had small iron balconies off the dining rooms, although the inclusion of only one interior stair forced the use of exterior fire escapes, detracting from the building's graciousness. The easterly line of apartments was duplexed, with the bedrooms one floor higher than the front rooms, although not directly above them. During the depression of the thirties the entire building was altered to provide smaller, more marketable units.

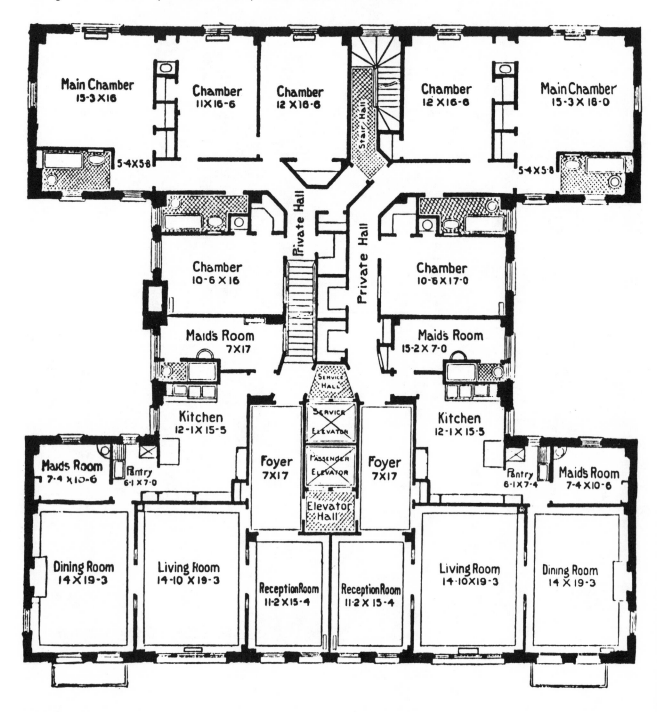

1 Lexington Avenue

Architect:	Herbert Lucas
Builder:	Edward Corning Company
Built:	1910

This building, constructed as an answer to those who wanted to live on Gramercy Park but who couldn't afford the cost of a private house there, provides spacious simplex and duplex apartments, such as the one illustrated below. Although Mayor Abram Hewitt's house next door and architect Stanford White's house across the street have since been razed, the building and its neighborhood still retain their gracious ambience.

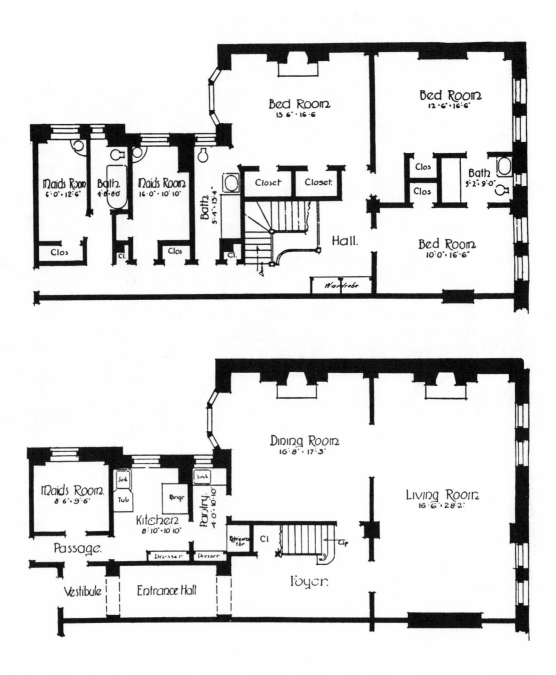

The Riviera
790 Riverside Drive

Architect: Rouse and Goldstone
Builder: Riviera Realty Company
Built: 1910

The Riviera might be regarded as one of the first apartment houses to cater to middle-class tenants with upper-class pretensions. The apartments, which range in size from 5 to 10 rooms, have such luxury features as libraries, separate butlers' pantries, and parquet flooring. However, the room sizes are merely adequate and the closet space is minimal. To obtain maximum usage of the available site, the architect was forced to string the apartments out along a many-cornered public corridor. The private halls in each suite are also excessively long and contorted. Nonetheless, there is an attempt at stylish decoration in limestone and terra cotta on the façade, which lends some interest to an otherwise ordinary building. The entrance lobby, shown in the two small photographs, was typical of the period. The carpets, the festoons, and the uniformed attendants have long since vanished.

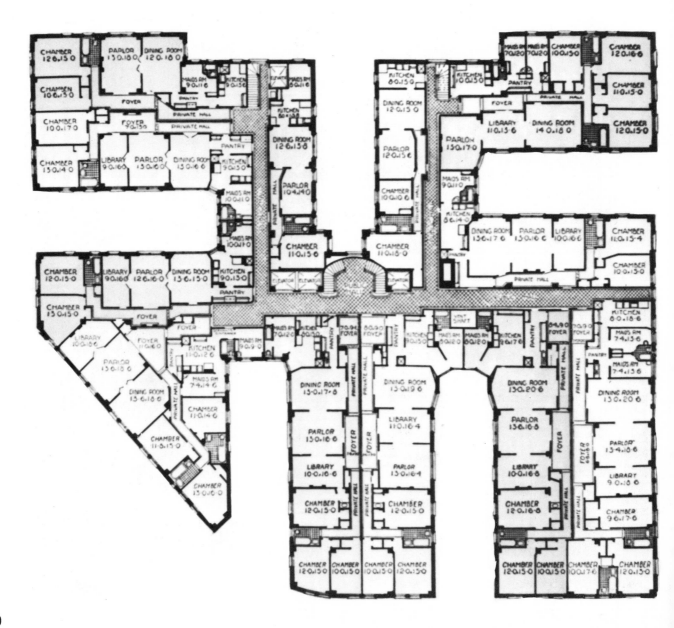

563 Park Avenue

Architect: Walter B. Chambers
Builder: William J. Taylor
Built: 1910, co-op

The exterior of **563 Park** is articulated on alternate floors with belt courses of white stone which, together with the obviously high and low ceiling heights on the alternate levels, would seem to indicate that the interior is composed entirely of duplex units. But while the apartments facing the avenue, as shown in the plans below, are indeed double-storied, those in the back are not. It would seem that in 1910 the concept of the exterior of a building reflecting its interior functions had not yet gained favor, at least in New York.

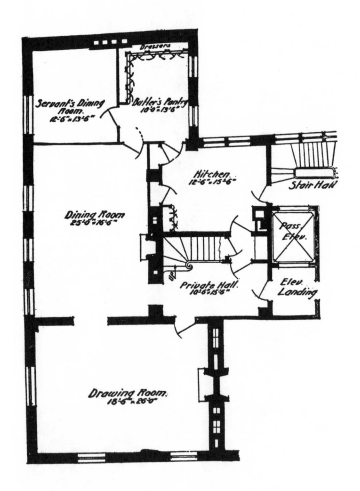

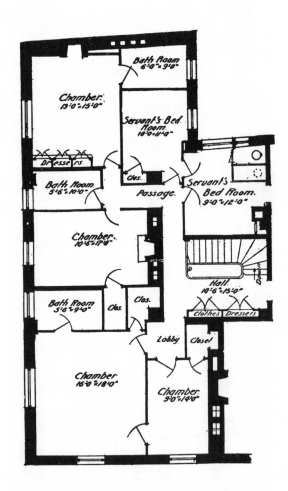

998 Fifth Avenue

Architect: McKim, Mead and White
Builder: Lee and Fleishman
Built: 1910, rental
Converted to co-op: 1953

998 was designed to cater to the needs of men who had always owned spacious town houses but who were concerned about the rising costs of maintaining them. At first renting was slow, the monied classes being reluctant to share a roof with others, even of their own kind. The agent, young Douglas L. Elliman, felt that one well-known tenant would draw others. Accordingly, he offered Senator Elihu Root a cut-rate to move from his large brick house at 71st Street and Park Avenue: $15,000 per year instead of $25,000. The Senator moved, followed by others of his class, starting Mr. Elliman on a very successful career.

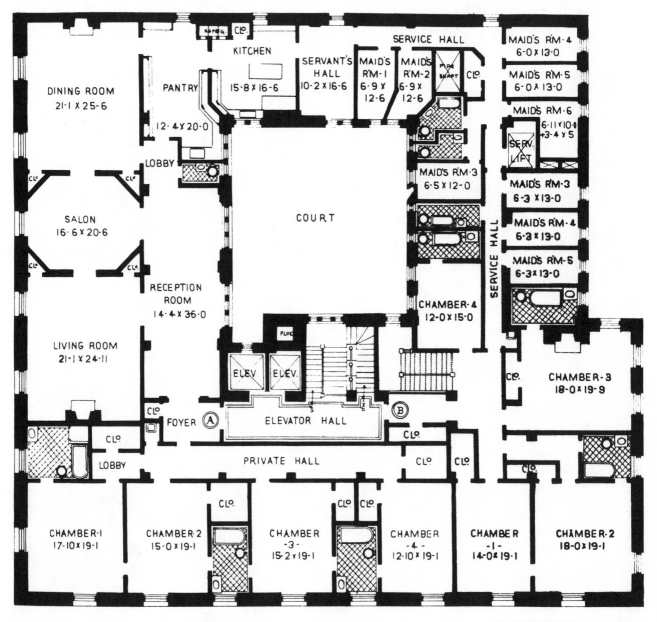

PLAN OF SECOND FLOOR

12 East 87th Street

Architect: George and Edward Blum
Builder: Capital Realty and Construction Company
Built: 1910
Remodelled: 1935, 1943

The façade is a modest one of brick and terra cotta, but the interior of this building once housed eight families in the space that now provides for four times that number. Originally there was only one apartment per floor, with 14 rooms and 4 baths. Particularly noteworthy were the four main rooms, each with a fireplace, which could open, one upon the other, to provide an entertaining space 42 feet by 50.

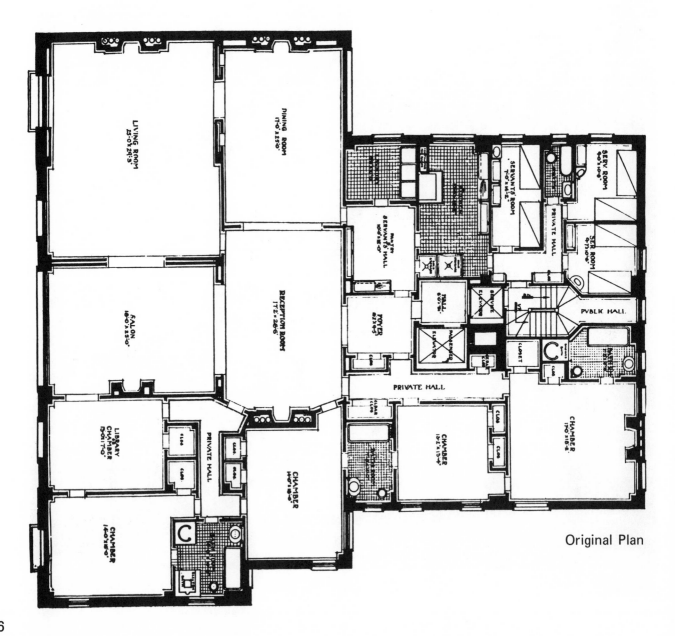

Original Plan

The Evanston
610 West End Avenue
272 West 90th Street

Architect: George and Edward Blum
Builder: 89th and 90th Company
Built: 1911

The bland and rather conventional façade of this building conceals a very curious floor plan which, surprisingly, has been changed only slightly over the years. Two of the apartments on each floor were duplexed, the sleeping rooms one floor higher than the entertaining rooms, but not directly over them. This enabled each apartment to provide the feeling of a private house while keeping costs down by providing identical arrangements on each floor (except, of course, at the top and the bottom.) Each of these apartments has a foyer plus a huge reception room (complete with fireplace but no window) bigger than any other room in the house. The back apartments shared this arrangement, providing a *front parlor* as well as the original of our present-day *family room*. This allowed the middle-class housewife to maintain a showroom for entertaining special guests and holding court while still having an everyday *living room.* Some of these apartments have since been subdivided into smaller units.

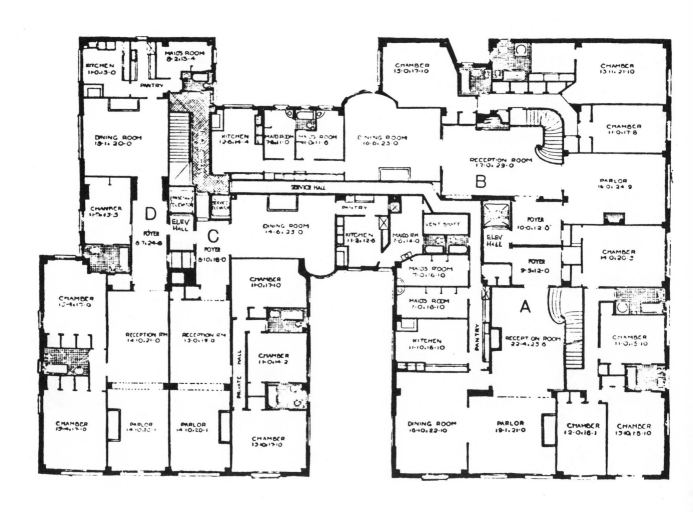

Marc Antony and Prince Humbert
514 and 520 Cathedral Parkway

Architect: Schwartz and Gross
Builder: Paterno Construction Company
Built: 1911

It is interesting to see how an architect of sixty-odd years ago treated the problem of providing a variety of apartment sizes and arrangements on a large lot, while still giving each a front exposure. Each of these two similar buildings is handled in a slightly different way, yielding five basic layouts, one of which includes a curious U-shaped hallway. Typical of many of the buildings of this period and class, the hallways are generally contorted and the closet space completely inadequate by our standards. Nonetheless the rooms, while minimal in size, are generally well-proportioned and arranged for ease of furniture placement.

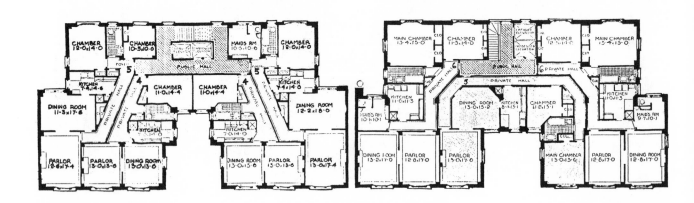

Heathcote Hall
609 West 114th Street

Architect: **Schwartz and Gross**
Builder: **Carnegie Construction Company**
Built: **1911**

Typifying the hollow-square form of mid-block apartment houses built in the early years of this century, each floor of this building is comprised of three small rear apartments and four larger *long hall* front apartments. The room sizes are minimal and the layouts awkward, but the building's proximity to Columbia University and to Riverside Park is a distinct advantage. Original rents ranged upward from $45 per month.

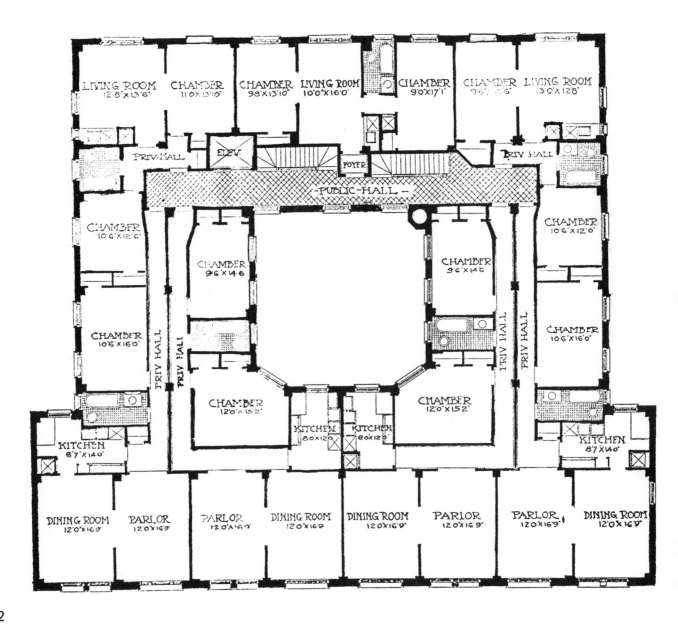

635 Park Avenue

Architect:	J.E.R.Carpenter
Builder:	S.Fullerton Weaver
Built:	1912

The present **635 Park Avenue** stands on the site of an earlier apartment house constructed in 1887 to designs of Henry Janeway Hardenbergh. **635** is quite uneventful from the outside, but it boasts a particularly fine plan, allotting one apartment of 13 rooms and 4 baths to a floor. Each apartment is divided into three sections: public, private and service. The three public or entertaining rooms, together with the circular entrance foyer, can easily be shut off from the private or sleeping rooms. The service spaces are situated so as to be convenient to both the public and private areas. Besides this functional separation, particular care was given to the proportions of the rooms, the placement of doors, and the holding of corridors to a minimum.

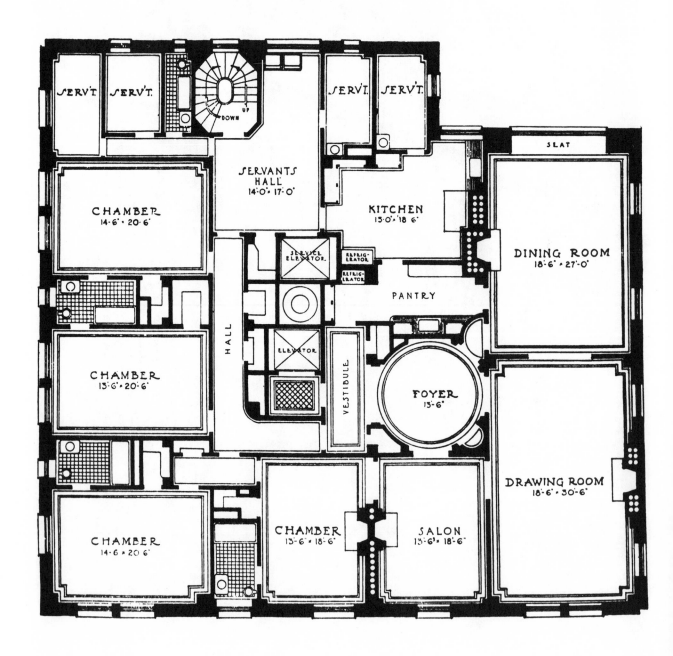

960 Park Avenue

As planned: **1910**
Architect: **Howells and Stokes**
Builder: **Dudley Construction Company**
As built: **1912**
Architect: **J.E.R.Carpenter**
Builder: **S.Fullerton Weaver**

960 was originally planned as an approximation of an Italian renaissance palace and contained 54 majestic cooperative apartments of 9 to 13 rooms, with 18 suites being duplexes and 3 suites triplexes. The apartments were exceptionally well laid out, with the major entertaining rooms arranged *en suite* around an entrance hall and the bedrooms equally well arranged. The absence of long halls and the care given the planning of the service spaces resulted in apartments of particularly gracious mien. The prospectus called for sale prices of $24,000 to $52,000 with average maintenance charges ranging from $245 to $420 per month. It mentioned that the soon-to-be-constructed Lexington Avenue Subway would add to the convenience of the building's location. As actually built, **960** occupies half the original lot with a more conventional luxury apartment house of twelve stories. This structure was designed with two apartments to a floor, but most of these have since been cut in half.

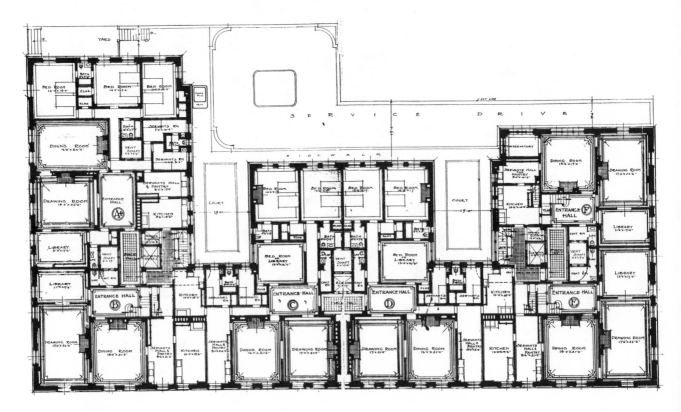

As Planned

As Planned

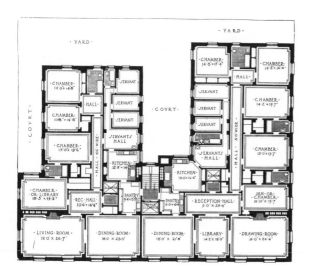

As Built

As Built

410 Park Avenue

Architect: Julius Harder
Builder: Cauldwell-Wingate Company
Built: 1914
Razed: 1956

410 was one of about 15 luxury buildings located south of 59th Street which have been torn down since World War II to make room for office buildings. The steel skeleton of one, number 430, still serves as the supporting structure for a modern office building, and all but one of the rest are gone. Each typical floor of **410** included two apartments, of 11 and 13 rooms apiece. The upper floors each contained a single apartment of 18 rooms and 8 baths, having a 77-foot sweep from the library to the living room. The building was typical of many of that period in that its refined and understated exterior belied its luxurious interior appointments.

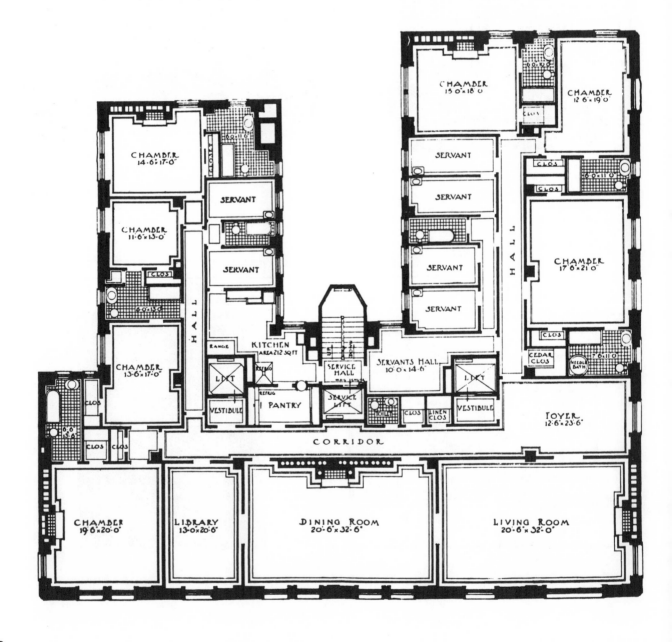

Hotel des Artistes
1 West 67th Street

Architect: George Mort Pollard
Builder: Walter Russell
Built: 1916

The name of this building is deceptive, as **1 West 67th Street** has always been a cooperative apartment house rather than a hotel. Nonetheless, it was designed to provide many of the amenities of a hotel, including a communal kitchen, a restaurant, squash courts, a swimming pool, a theater and a ballroom. The kitchen has been converted to small apartments and the theater and ballroom now serve as television studio space, but a grand and gracious ambience still pervades the building. Most of the building's apartments include double-height living rooms and balcony bedrooms, and some are graced with elaborate English tudor gothic detailing and huge stone fireplaces. The exterior detailing is particularly fanciful, with carved stone figures representing the arts.

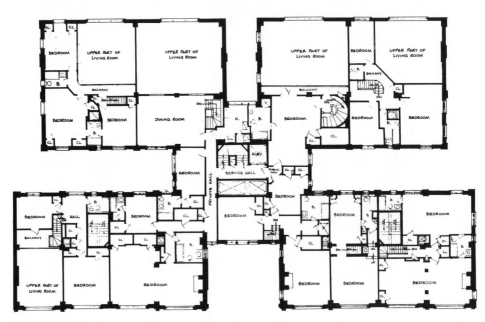

8th Floor Mezzanine

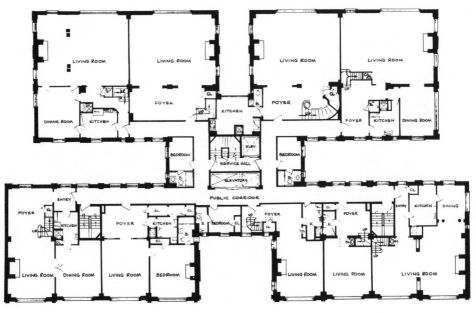

8th Floor

820 Fifth Avenue

Architect: Starrett and Van Vleck
Builder: Fred T. Ley Company
Built: 1916

820 Fifth Avenue is one of the few luxury apartment buildings left in the city whose huge suites have never been subdivided. It retains its original detailing, and the care with which it was originally maintained has been continued. Each apartment, occupying an entire floor, is grandly arranged around a 44-foot entrance gallery and includes 5 bedrooms, 6½ bathrooms and 7 servants' rooms as well as the usual entertaining rooms. Five fireplaces are provided, and the kitchen is equipped with four sinks.

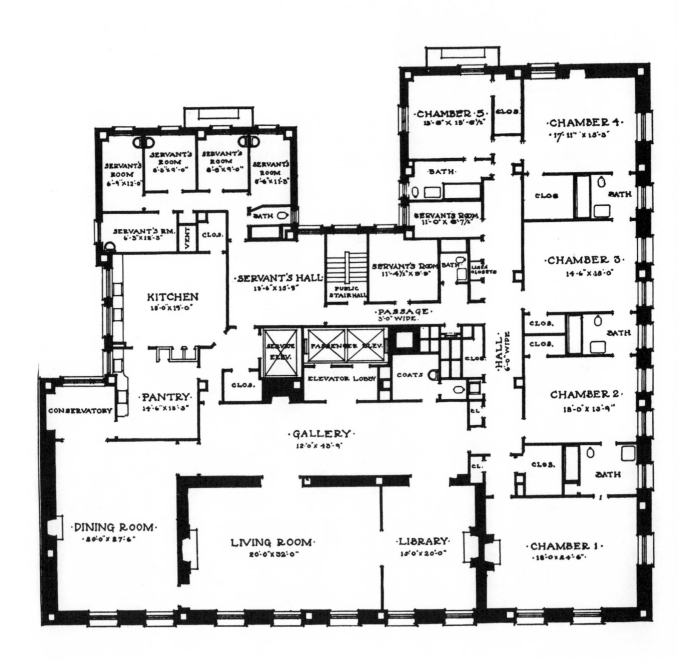

907 Fifth Avenue

Architect:	J.E.R.Carpenter
Builder:	907 Fifth Avenue Company
Built:	1916
Remodelled:	1950-1960
Architect:	Seigel and Green
Builder:	November Realty Corporation

This building originally contained very spacious apartments, no more than two to a floor, the largest consisting of 28 rooms and renting for $30,000 per year. The changing real estate market after World War II necessitated the conversion of these suites into smaller units in order to maintain an acceptable financial return. In the case of **907**, this was accomplished gradually, as apartments became vacant, thus preserving the essential character of the building. This was in marked contrast to what was done across the street at number 910, described on the next page, where the building was stripped to the steelwork and totally rebuilt, losing in the process all that gave the original building its distinction and beauty.

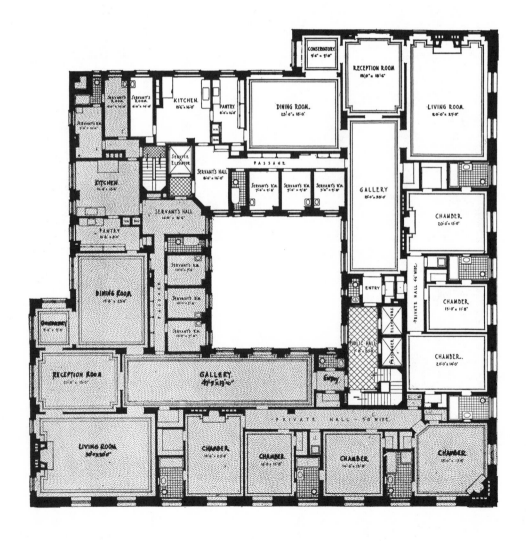

910 Fifth Avenue

Architect:	Fred F. French Company
Builder:	Fred F. French Company
Built:	1920
Rebuilt:	1959
Architect:	Sylvan Bien
	Robert L. Bien
Builder:	Pador Realty Corporation

In 1920, living styles among the rich included large entertainment spaces along with the live-in servants to maintain them. Forty years later most people had neither the money nor the inclination to maintain such elaborate domiciles. This change has led to generally smaller apartments with fewer bedrooms and nearly no maids' rooms. A comparison of the earlier and later plans of **910 Fifth Avenue** will reveal how this change was accomplished within the framework of the existing steel skeleton of the earlier building. The photograph shows the original façade of the building. Its present appearance is unworthy of pictorial documentation.

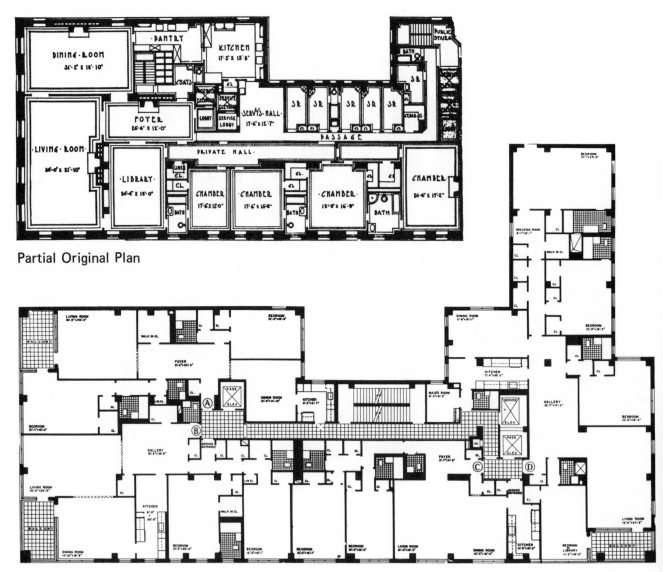

Partial Original Plan

Plan as Rebuilt

4 East 66th Street
845 Fifth Avenue

Architect:	**J.E.R.Carpenter**
Builder:	**William Henry Barnum**
Built:	**1920, co-op**

In contrast to the stark severity of the exterior, the interior of **4 East 66th** is grandly elegant, and as with 820 Fifth Avenue, virtually unchanged. Each floor contains one apartment of 18 rooms, including 6 bedrooms and two huge entertaining rooms overlooking Central Park. The ceilings in these apartments are unusually high—about 12 feet—and the decorative details are especially well-wrought. The windows of the 35-foot entrance gallery to each apartment now overlook the adjacent Temple Emanuel, where once stood the twin houses of John Jacob Astor and his mother, Mrs. William Astor.

898 Park Avenue

Architect: **John Sloan and Adolph E. Nast**
Builder: **Leddy and Moore for the Madel-Ehirch Corporation**
Built: **1924**

This handsome building, decorated in a Lombardy Romanesque manner with added grotesque heads and figures, originally contained duplex apartments exclusively, with each suite occupying two full floors as shown below. In 1948, architect Simon Zelnick converted each duplex into two simplex apartments leaving, however, the 5th and 6th floor and the 14th and penthouse suites intact. The exterior brick-work was recently restored to its original golden-hued sparkle, but the elaborately wrought entrance doors gave way to a more practical but mundane set made of aluminum.

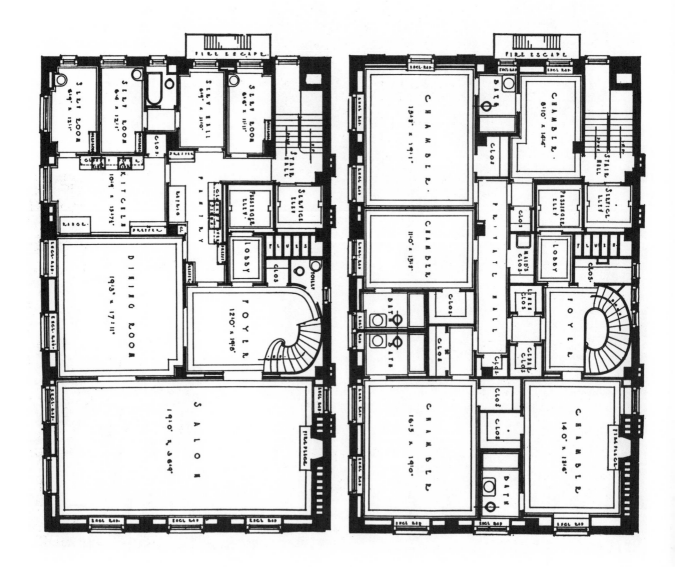

1020 Fifth Avenue

Architect:	Warren and Wetmore
Builder:	Michael E. Paterno
Built:	1925, co-op

Careful detailing in limestone gives this building an air of refined elegance. Its special distinction, however, lies in the arrangement of its apartments. An interesting variety of spacious accommodations is provided, including a duplex maisonette of 12 rooms, simplex apartments, and a duplex penthouse of 17 rooms with 7½ baths. The cross-sectional diagram shows how some of the apartments, including the one shown in plan, were given a living room with an extra-high ceiling. Original prices ranged from $40,000 to $150,000 with monthly maintenance charges of $410 to $1,540.

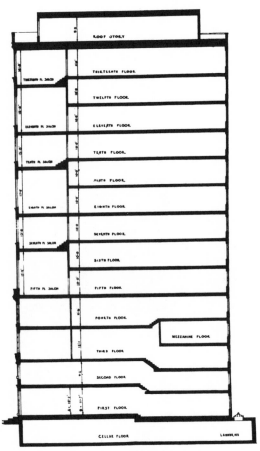

Cross Section Plan Showing Ceiling Heights

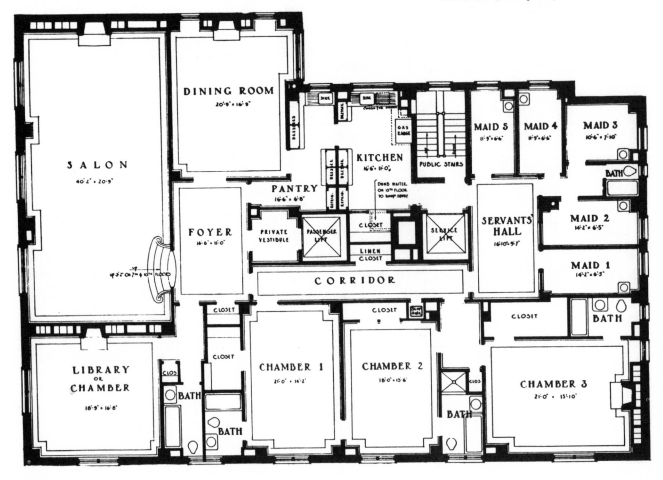

956 Fifth Avenue

As planned:	**1923**
Architect:	**I.N.Phelps Stokes**
Builder:	**956 Fifth Avenue, Inc.**
As built:	**1925**
Architect:	**Nathan Korn**
Builder:	**HRH Construction Company**

The rendering on the facing page shows an 8-story building at **956 Fifth Avenue** originally planned as an interpretation of a domestic building of the Italian renaissance, adapted to the needs of an apartment house. This represented the then-prevalent attitude of upper-class families that apartment living was a necessary evil to be tolerated only if the pretense of living in a private house could be maintained. For this reason, duplex suites and very spacious simplex flats were particularly popular. Although the original venture provided these, the small number of apartments in the building rendered the scheme impractical. Instead, a 14-story building was erected with one apartment per floor. Around 1950, several apartments were subdivided to provide two units per floor.

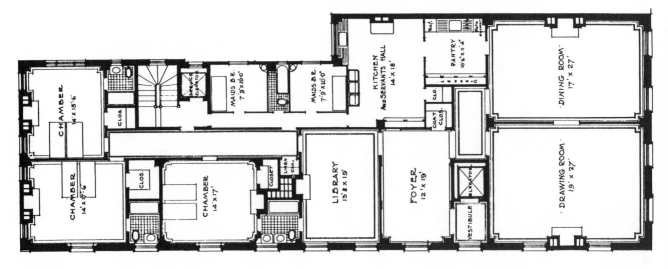

As Planned

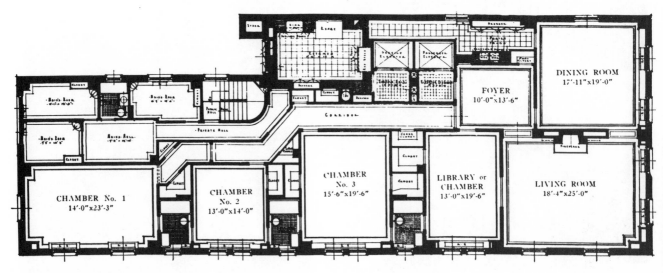

As Originally Built

31 East 79th Street

Architect:	**G.B.Beaumont**
Builder:	**William H. Rowan**
Built:	**1925 and 1928, co-op**

The original section of this building consists of one 7-room apartment to a floor, well-planned and carefully detailed. Far more interesting, however, is the westerly portion of the building, built three years later. It replaced a typical New York brownstone residence with a building that reproduced the original brownstone's triplex plan four times, one on top of the other! Presumably this was meant to provide an apartment for the previous owner of the brownstone, in the manner of Mrs. E.F. Hutton's suite at 1107 Fifth Avenue, described on the next page.

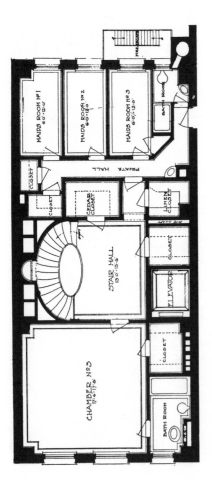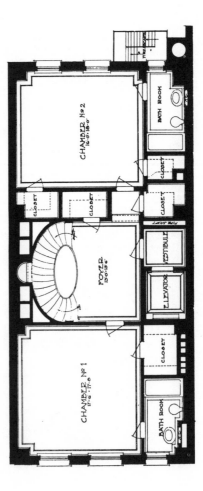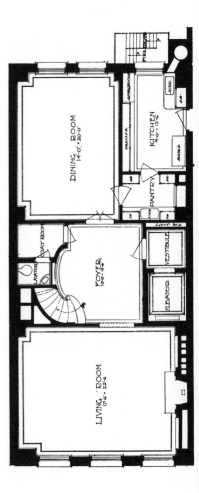

1107 Fifth Avenue

Architect: Rouse and Goldstone
Builder: George A. Fuller Company
Built: 1926

The erection of this house was directly related to the willingness of Mrs. E.F. Hutton to agree to sell her townhouse property site, but only if the builder would virtually recreate her house atop the apartment structure. The result was the 54-room triplex shown, which was certainly the largest and very possibly the most luxurious apartment ever created anywhere. It was served by a private carriage driveway on 92nd Street and a private elevator as well as a separate ground floor suite for a concierge. The apartment included a silver room, a wine room and cold-storage rooms for flowers and for furs along with a self-contained suite of rooms for Mrs. Hutton's parents, Mr. and Mrs. Post. The annual rental was $75,000, which was paid for the term of the 15-year lease. Subsequently, after the apartment had remained vacant for ten years, the triplex was converted into six smaller, but still luxurious, 9-room apartments.

PENTHOUSE

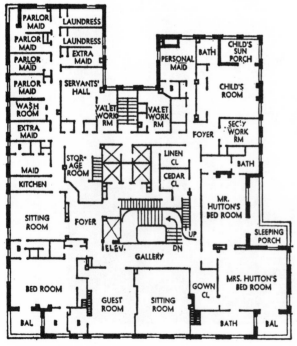

13 TH FLOOR

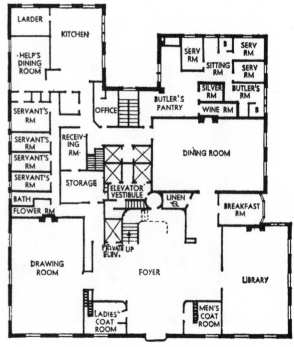

12 TH FLOOR

1107 FIFTH AVENVE

109

As befitted the largest apartment in New York, the rooms of the Hutton suite were decorated in a grand manner that one might more likely expect to find in a mansion at Newport or an estate on the North Shore. Nonetheless, by legal definition the building at 1107 Fifth Avenue was classed as a tenement house. Equally surprising is the fact that this grandeur was provided in a rental apartment rather than in a cooperative.

Mrs. Hutton's Bathroom

The Breakfast Room

Mrs. Hutton's Bedroom

The Nursery

The Drawing Room

The Foyer

The Dining Room

The Library

The Daughters' Sitting Room

Mr. Hutton's Sitting Room

35 West 9th Street

Architect: **Townsend, Steinle and Haskell**
Builder: **35 West 9th Street Corporation**
Built: **1926**

This building is typical of hundreds of side-street apartment houses built between 1915 and 1930. Such buildings were generally built on lots 70 to 100 feet wide, were 9 to 15 stories in height and H-shaped in plan. **35 West 9th** is slightly different from most in that the four apartments on each floor are not designed as two mirror-image pairs but instead are arranged in four different layouts. By this time two elevators and two sets of interior stairs were standard, and gas-lights were included only in the stair halls for emergency use.

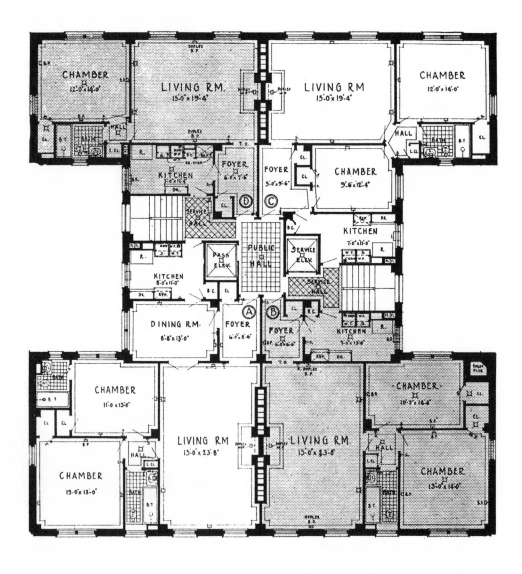

113

The Beresford
211 Central Park West
1 and 7 West 81st Street

Architect:	**Emery Roth**
Builder:	**HRH Construction Company**
Built:	**1929**
Converted to co-op:	**1962**

Known as much for its distinguished tenants, many from show business, as for its architectural appearance, **The Beresford** has presented a striking silhouette on the north corner of 81st Street since it replaced an earlier hotel of the same name. It provides large apartments with spacious rooms, extensive storage facilities and elegant appointments. Entrance is provided through several separate lobbies handsomely detailed in marble and bronze. **The Beresford**, along with the San Remo at 145 Central Park West, was the last of the lavish New York apartment houses designed in the classical manner so favored in the early part of the twentieth century. The high level of maintenance over the years, together with its convenient location and relatively secure co-operative status, assure it of a long life.

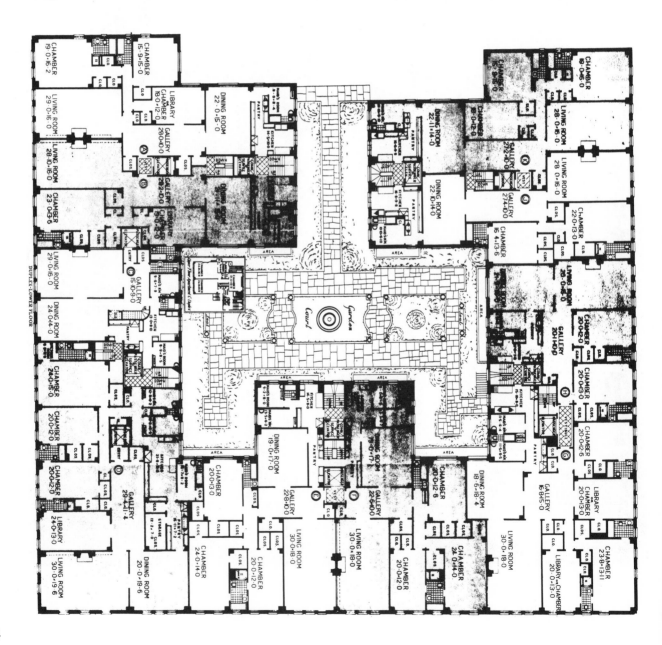

1185 Park Avenue

Architect: Schwartz and Gross
Builder: Bricken Construction Company
Built: 1929
Converted to co-op: 1953

1185 Park was the last of the large apartment houses built in the shape of a hollow square, an arrangement utilized in the design of Graham Court, The Belnord and The Apthorp. Careful design, utilizing six separate lobbies, enabled each elevator to serve only two apartments. This, together with the spacious entrance galleries and the thoughtful arrangement of the rooms, afforded each suite a particular gracious ambience. The plan shown is of one of the most luxurious of these, a unique duplex penthouse. The photograph, taken about 1936, shows the gothicised ornament and the triple-arched entrance to the interior court. Note also the canvas awnings at many of the windows. Used before the advent of air-conditioning to keep apartments cool, they were eventually banned as a fire hazard.

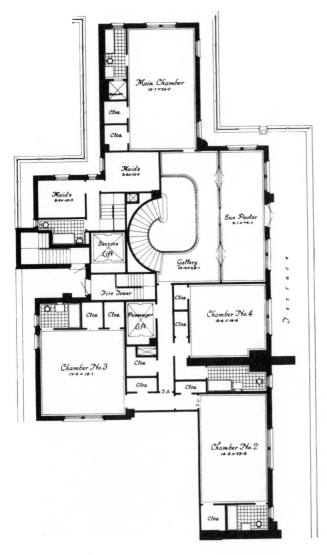

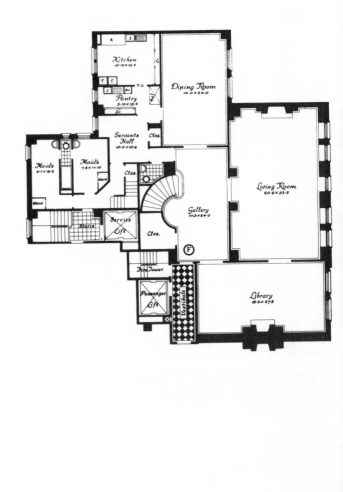

116

1215 Fifth Avenue

Architect: Schultze and Weaver
Builder: Thompson Starrett Company
for Arthur Brisbane
Built: 1929

Number 1215 is a colorful building with modified romanesque detailing, built by Arthur Brisbane, one-time columnist for the Hearst newspaper chain. On the 14th, 15th and penthouse floors, a very large apartment was included for his own use. Shown below are the plans for its two lower floors. Along with numerous bedrooms and baths, a study and a library, was a rooftop greenhouse, a two-storied dining hall 33 feet long, and a two-storied living room 60 feet long with a baronial fireplace at each end! Serving this apartment was a private entrance hall on the first floor and a private elevator. After Brisbane died in 1936 and the building's mortgage was foreclosed in 1939, the apartment was subdivided into several smaller units.

119

55 Central Park West

Architect: Schwartz and Gross
Builder: Earle and Calhoun
Built: 1929
Converted to co-op: 1967

Stylistically, **55 Central Park West** was an innovative building, utilizing modernistic forms and a brick façade carefully color-graded from deep red at the base to pale beige at the top. The typical floors, illustrated below, each contain 7 apartments ranging in size from 3 to 6 rooms. Each of the living rooms is set two steps below the other rooms, lending the air of a private house to each unit. The apartments are well laid out, with good sized entrance galleries and minimal hall space. Closet space is adequate and false fireplaces are provided. The upper set-back floors have several larger apartments (up to 9 rooms and 4 baths) with narrow terraces.

960 Fifth Avenue

Architect:	Rosario Candela
	Warren and Wetmore
Builder:	Anthony Campagna
Built:	1929, partially co-op

960 Fifth Avenue, built on the site of the 130-room mansion of Senator William Clark, is a luxurious residence of restrained elegance, containing very large, very expensive apartments. Through a careful dovetailing of the different units, the entertaining rooms were provided with extra-high ceilings while the remainder of each suite was of normal height. One of the original apartments was a 17-room suite sold to Dr. Preston Pope Satterwhite for $450,000, the highest price ever paid up to that time. Recently the building reasserted its financial exclusivity when the apartment shown in plan was sold by the estate of Mrs. Ailsa Mellon Bruce for $900,000. Fronting on 77th Street is a separate section of the building containing rental apartments.

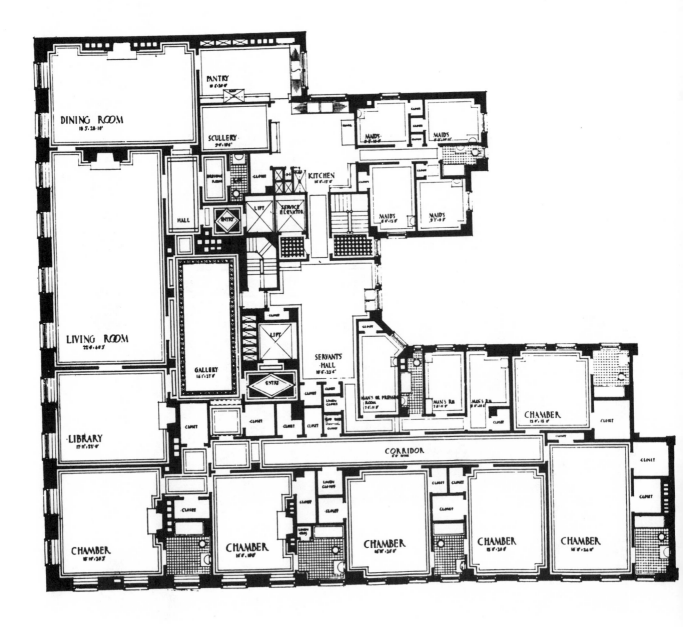

London Terrace
9th to 10th Avenues, 23rd to 24th Streets

Architect:	**Farrar and Watmaugh**
Builder:	**Henry Mandel**
Built:	**1930**

At the time of its completion this 14-building 1700-unit complex was described as *the greatest single residential development the world has ever seen.* Although shorn of some of its glory by the construction of other large projects in later years, it still maintains a massive dignity. The ten mid-block buildings, of which a typical floor plan is shown below, contain studio and one-bedroom apartments while the four corner structures house larger units. Tenants are served by an internal telephone system and share an olympic-sized swimming pool as well as a secluded courtyard garden and a sundeck with a fine view of the Hudson. Prior to 1929, about 400 people—a good many of them artists and writers—lived in the 80-odd houses on the block-square site. The houses formerly on 23rd Street had been built in 1845, patterned on the fashionable London row houses of that time. Collectively they were called London Terrace, from which the present complex took its name.

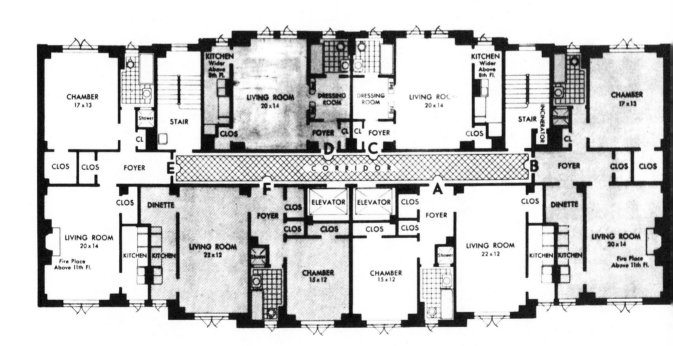

River House
447 East 52nd Street

Architect:	**Bottomly, Wagner and White**
Builder:	**James Stewart and Company**
Built:	**1930, co-op**

River House represented a strong confidence in the basic economic health of the city, built as it was on the heels of the 1929 crash of the stock market. It contains some of the most luxurious apartments ever built, including large simplexes and duplexes, and a triplex with a huge double-height living room. Physically part of the apartment house, although a separate corporate entity, is the River Club, occupying five floors of the building. It presently includes a swimming pool, tennis courts and a gymnasium along with dining and entertaining spaces as well as 21 bedrooms. Before the FDR Drive was built, around 1941, the building fronted directly on the East River and had its own yacht mooring. The building's tenants have always been a particularly exclusive group, including leading figures from business and the arts, with a heavy concentration of New York's most socially prominent names.

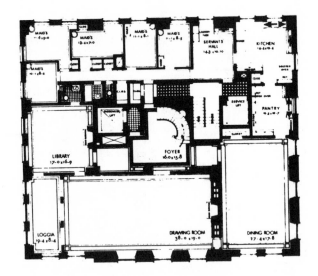 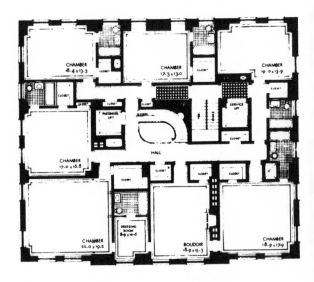

The Majestic
115 Central Park West

Architect: Irwin S. Chanin
            Jacques Delamarre
Builder: Chanin Construction Company
Built: 1930
Converted to co-op: 1957

The Majestic, built on the site of Alfred Zucker's 1894 Hotel Majestic, was originally designed with apartments ranging in size from 11 to 24 rooms after a study of apartment accommodations in New York indicated that suites of this size were most in demand. When the steelwork for the building had been partially erected, the stock market crashed and along with it the market for palatial residences. A frantic reworking of the plans resulted in a new assortment of apartment sizes ranging from very small units to ones of 14 rooms. Special features included cantilevered construction at the corners of the Central Park frontage which enabled glass-walled solaria to be placed at these points. In addition to these enclosed porches, a large solarium was provided on the 19th floor for the general use of all tenants in the building. Sculptor Rene Chanbellan's design of the building's futuristic forms, the interior decoration, and the furnishings were originally described as *Modern American* but are now generally referred to as *Moderne.* It was an answer to the European-inspired revival styles then in vogue. The mode was characteristic of the thirties, but looks sadly dated today.

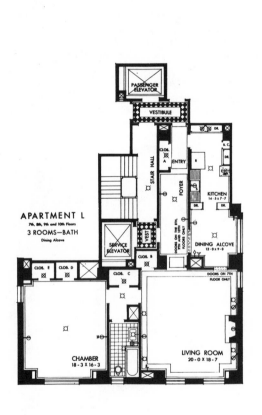

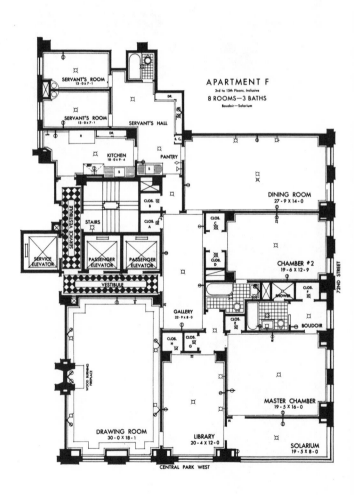

The Century Apartments
25 Central Park West

Architect: Irwin S. Chanin
               Jacques Delamarre
Builder: Chanin Construction Company
Built: 1931

The Century Apartments replaced Carrère and Hastings' ill-fated Century Theatre, shown in the small photograph. Designed to appeal to people who had given up larger apartments, it offered 52 varieties of accommodations ranging from a 1-room unit with a wrap-around terrace to an 11-room suite with a step-down living room and a private entrance from the street. It was the first building to provide the amenities of penthouse and duplex living to apartments as small as 3-rooms. The plan illustrated below shows this in the form of a one-bedroom apartment in which the sleeping quarters are on an upper level, although not directly above the living area. Other notable features of the building include a then-new form of concrete construction that obviated the need for beam-drops in the ceilings, cantilevered floor slabs to eliminate corner columns and to provide additional width to the terraces, and special window glass capable of transmitting the ultra-violet rays of sunlight.

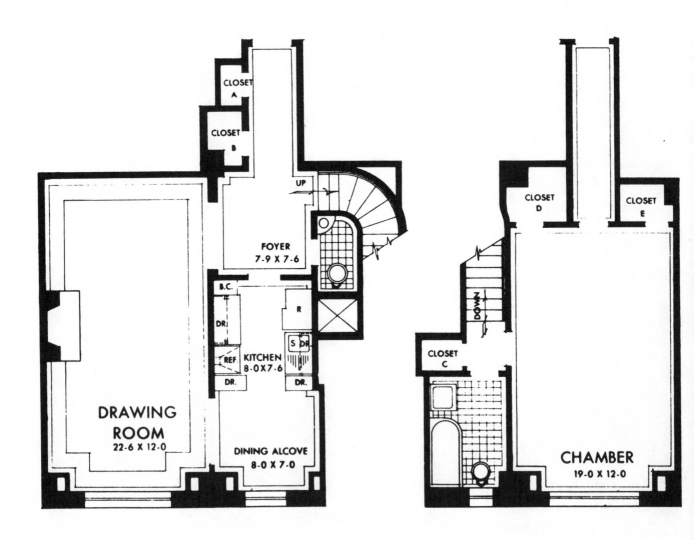

625 Park Avenue

Architect: J.E.R.Carpenter
Builder: Louis Kaufman
Built: 1931
Converted to co-op: 1968

The special distinction of this building lies in its 26-room triplex penthouse. The plans below show how that apartment appeared during its 30-year ownership by Madame Helena Rubenstein, although it has since been renovated for another of cosmetics' crown families, that of Revlon's Charles Revson. Madame Rubenstein had apartments in Paris and London as well as country estates in America, but she always considered **625 Park** as *home*. Housed there was her extensive and exceedingly eclectic collections of art and jewelry. The apartment was a very personalized reflection of a very individual-istic woman, and contained, among the more unusual things, a special room designed to house a collection of ultra-miniature furniture in glass-enclosed dioramas, a 68-foot long room used for parties and chamber music recitals, and another room of no particular purpose other than to house a set of Venetian shell furniture and a series of murals painted directly on the walls by Salvador Dali.

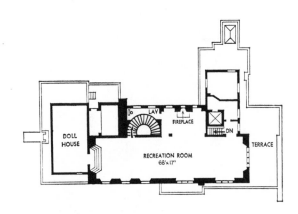

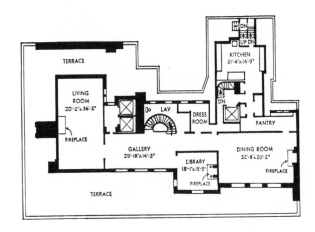

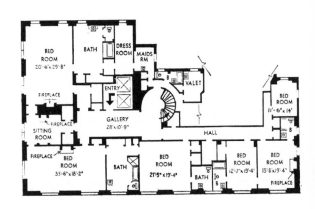

120 East End Avenue

Architect: Charles A. Platt
Builder: George A. Fuller Company for Vincent Astor
Built: 1931, co-op

This limestone-faced and quietly understated building was built as substantial investment property catering to people of means with large families. Located close to a pleasant park and containing large apartments with up to 7 bedrooms and 6 servants' rooms, it was meant to afford a good environment for families with many children. The typical floors have three apartments each, of 10, 11 and 14 rooms. Units on the upper floors range in size from 3 to 19 rooms, and 5 duplexes are included. All the suites are exceptionally well laid-out, with lavishly spacious entertaining areas and carefully thought-out circulation and service spaces. Vincent Astor, who built this house, reserved the entire 17th floor for his own apartment, which surprisingly still exists.

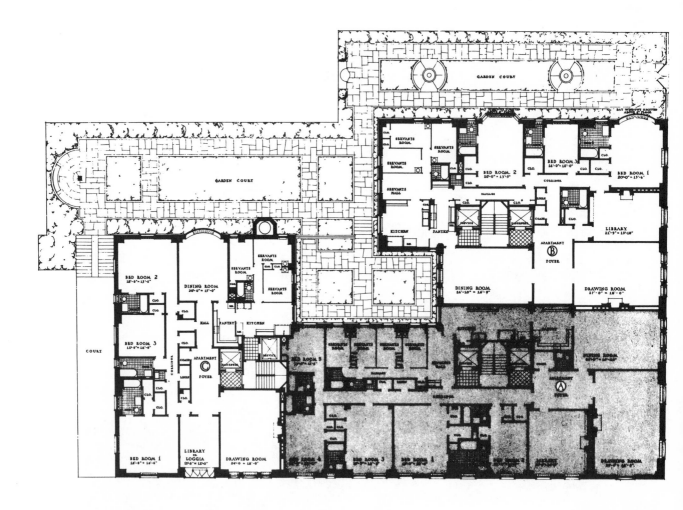

Butterfield House
37 West 12th Street

Architect: Mayer, Whittlesey and Glass
William J. Conklin
James S. Rossant
Builder: Daniel L. Gray
Built: 1962, co-op

Butterfield House is particularly notable for its sensitive and tasteful façade on 12th Street, carefully designed to blend with the surrounding townhouses. Erected prior to the enactment of the Landmarks Preservation Law, it nonetheless conforms admirably to the Law's features relating to Historic Districts, within one of which **37 West 12th Street** lies. Actually consisting of a small building on 12th Street connected to a much larger one on 13th, **Butterfield House** includes predominantly 2- and 3-bedroom apartments, many of which are arranged so that the living rooms face the street while the sleeping quarters overlook the quieter inner courtyard. Balconies and jalousied garden rooms are provided, along with a handsome garden between the two sections of the building.

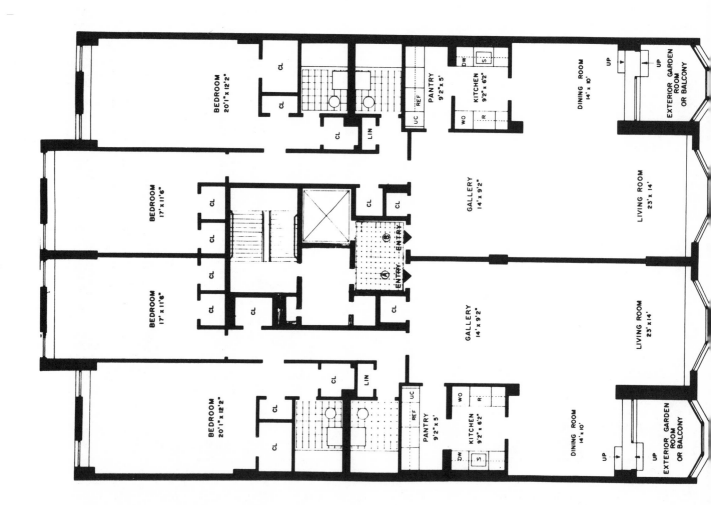

Tower East
190 East 72nd Street

Architect: **Emery Roth and Sons**
Builder: **Tishman Realty and Construction Company**
Built: **1962, leasehold co-op**

Tower East was the first apartment building to be built under the new zoning resolution as a sheer tower without any upper-floor set-backs. Containing 132 units, it sits on a one-story base which houses shops, a garage, and a 500-seat motion-picture theatre. Each floor consists of four apartments of various sizes, all with L-shaped corner living/dining rooms. There is a bathroom for each bedroom, but they are all windowless. Despite the light colored exposed-concrete exterior columns and walls, the building has a somber appearance, the result of the use of bronze colored window frames and dark-tinted glass.

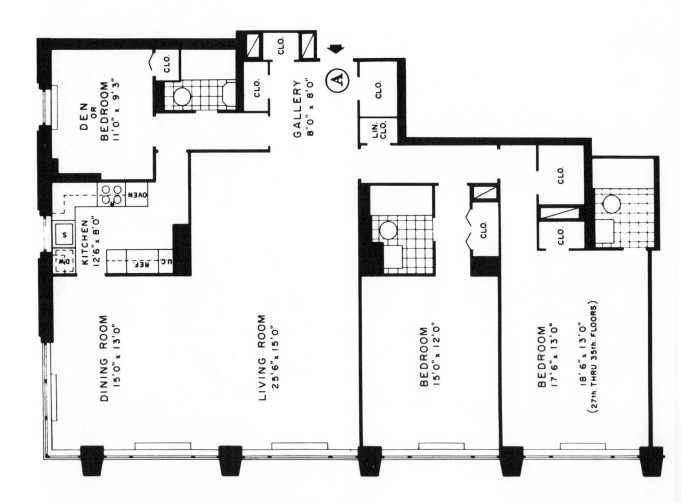

Kips Bay Plaza
333 East 30th Street
330 East 33rd Street

Architect: I. M. Pei
Builder: William Zeckendorf
Built: 1962

Kips Bay Plaza was built as a middle-income urban renewal project whose rents have long since exceeded middle-income limits. It was one of the first projects of the heavily-built fifties and sixties to treat the construction of an apartment house as a design problem rather than merely an exercise in maximizing the financial return by minimizing the project cost. As an early example of exposed cast-in-place concrete, extensive experiments were made to determine the best means of erecting the structure. The results are a pair of dramatically handsome buildings sharing a sympathetically landscaped site with a professional building and a small shopping center. The southerly building was erected first and served as a proving ground; several design elements were changed when the northerly unit was built. The floor plans are distinctive, providing large, square living rooms and good closet space. The bathrooms and kitchens are windowless, however, a defect which is partially offset by floor-to-ceiling doors which lend a slight air of additional spaciousness.

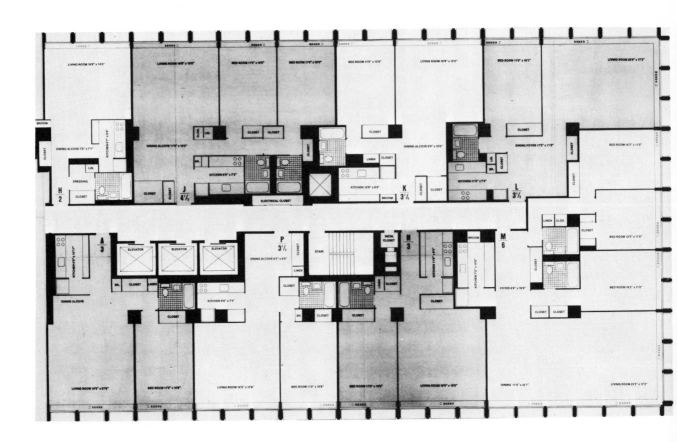

Premier Apartments
333 East 69th Street

Architect: Mayer, Whittlesey and Glass
                William J. Conklin
Builder: Daniel L. Gray
Built: 1963
Converted to co-op: 1974

This building is an unusual solution to the recurring problem of how to handle the long narrow mid-block lot. Crisply detailed and strongly articulated, the façade yields a playful contrast of light and shadow through a wall line which alternately advances and recedes. The lower two floors are devoted to duplex units which, with their private entrances and street-front gardens or private backyards, recall the nearby brownstones. The typical floors contain a variety of 1-, 2- and 3-bedroom apartments while the roof level is partially given over to a wind-protected sun deck and an enclosed recreation room, *a la* Le Corbusier's *Unité d'Habitation.*

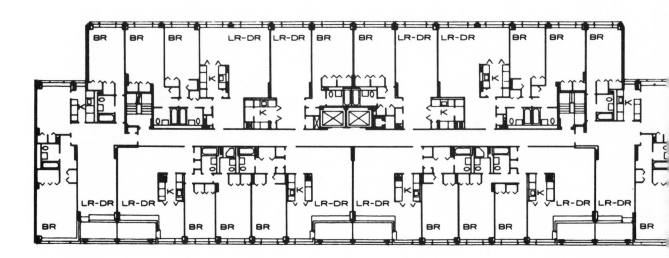

857 Fifth Avenue

Architect: Robert L. Bien
Builder: The Frouge Corporation
Built: 1963
Converted to co-op: 1968

857 represents a return to the privacy of one apartment to a floor and to the distinct separation of the private bedroom area from the more public entertaining rooms. For parties, the plan affords three very spacious main rooms all of which open onto a large entrance gallery. Two bathrooms are available in this area together with ample closet space. At the top of the building a palatial triplex has been constructed.   It is unfortunate that the exterior of **857** does not approach the quality of its interior. The façade is a gauche assemblage of disparate materials that contrasts sharply with its more sedate neighbors.

145

Chatham Towers
170 Park Row

Architect:	Kelly and Gruzen
Builder:	Association for Middle Income Housing
Built:	1964, co-op

This 240-unit project was built under Title I of the Federal Housing Act, for upper-middle income families. Two exposed-concrete towers surmount a 125-car garage on a triangular site near City Hall. Studio to 3-bedroom apartments are worked into a particularly compact plan which provides balconies on alternate floors. Two *firsts* for Manhattan are the windows, double-glazed with built-in venetian blinds, and the walls, two 1-inch layers of gypsum board with an air space between for sound control. Hailed by the professional critics for its neo-brutalist elegance, it has also evoked acerbic comments about its apparent incompleteness.

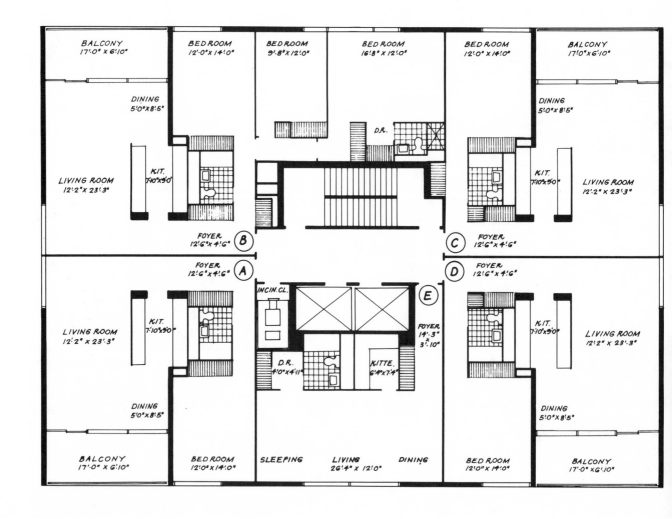

United Nations Plaza
49th Street, east of First Avenue

Architect:	Harrison and Abramovitz
Builder:	Alcoa Plaza Associates
Built:	1965, co-op

These two buildings, sitting on a common six-story base which contains commercial space, represent one of the more expensive and luxurious of newer apartment ventures. The units range in size from 3½ rooms with 1 bath to 9 rooms with 6½ baths. The apartments above the 31st floor are duplexes with curving staircases, wood-burning fireplaces and private elevators. Recognizing the variety of prospective owners' decorating tastes, the builders refrained from providing fireplace mantels, special electrical fixtures or wallcoverings within the apartments. On the other hand, for a uniform exterior appearance, they provided fiberglas draperies of a neutral color at all windows. Original prices for the apartments ranged from $27,600 to $166,000. Recent asking prices, however, have been considerably in excess of those figures.

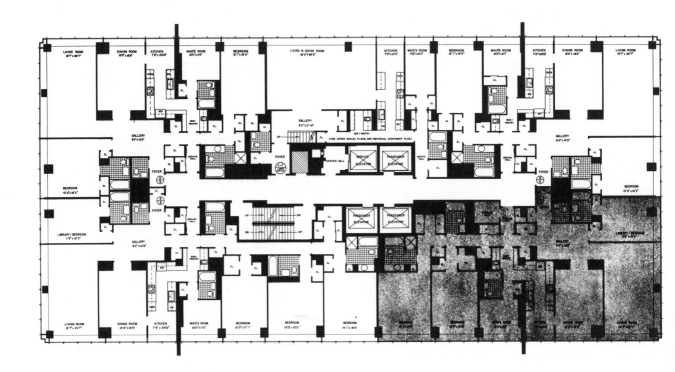

University Plaza
LaGuardia Place, Bleeker to Houston Streets

Architect: I. M. Pei
Builder: New York University
Built: 1966
One building: co-op
Two buildings: faculty housing

One to four-bedroom units are provided in three 30-story pinwheel-plan reinforced-concrete towers. Built on the site of a proposed-but-never-built triplet to the twin monoliths to the north, this project brings a crisply articulated elegance to an otherwise dreary area. Spacious apartments for middle-income families were provided, with an unusually high level of private and public amenity. All but the smallest units have two exposures and the larger apartments are given extra bathrooms. Closets are spacious as are the lofty ground floor lobbies and the underground garage. Of particular delight are the eyebrows over the windows which alleviate the need for shades or blinds, and are a result of the carefully detailed structural system. A giant sculpture by Pablo Picasso adds to the project's satisfaction of its residents' more-than-merely-basic needs.

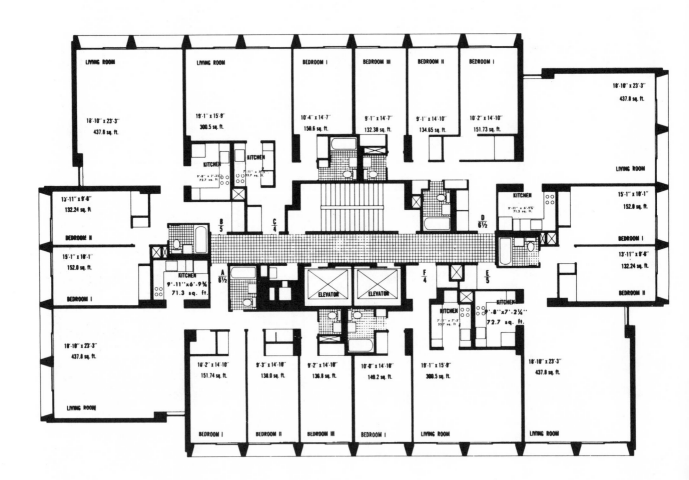

980 Fifth Avenue

Architect: Paul Resnick
            Harry F. Green
Builder: Gustave Ring
            Milton Ritzenberg
Built: 1966, co-op

980 Fifth, shown in the upper picture, replaced Isaac Brokaw's 1887 approximation of a French chateau, shown in the lower one. A comparison of the two photographs reveals that all that has remained of the graciousness, the respect for neighboring buildings, and the human scale of the earlier streetscape is naught but the fire hydrant. The new building offers large and expensive accommodations, the biggest being a 16-room duplex penthouse which originally cost $418,000. Many of the original details used throughout the building—gold-plated bathroom fixtures, bidets, domed ceilings—were removed by some of the 43 owner-occupants. The large number of changes suggests a stern re-evaluation of what people of means want in their apartments.

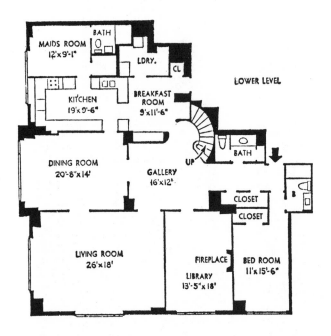

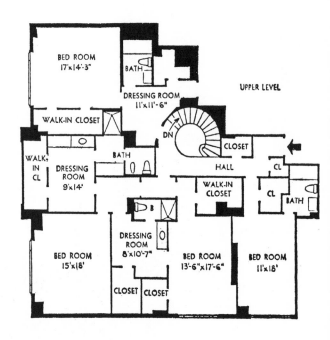

49 East 89th Street

Architect: The Office of Phillip Birnbaum
             Oppenheimer, Brady and Lehrecke
Builder: Rose Associates
Built: 1969

This building embodies a conventional floor plan of 2- and 3-bedroom apartments, each with a balcony and at least 2 bathrooms; the layout of a typical suite is shown. It offers amenities such as nine-foot ceilings (unusual for a new building), an electronic security system and especially sound-resistant construction. In addition, there is provided on the roof a year-'round swimming pool, sun deck, lounge, and lockers and sauna rooms for both men and women. The building's exceptional distinction, however, results from the tasteful elegance of its exterior. Carefully detailed in a mellow brick with bronze trim, the image conveyed is clean-lined and classically contemporary. Brick paving and brick planters add a note of warmth.

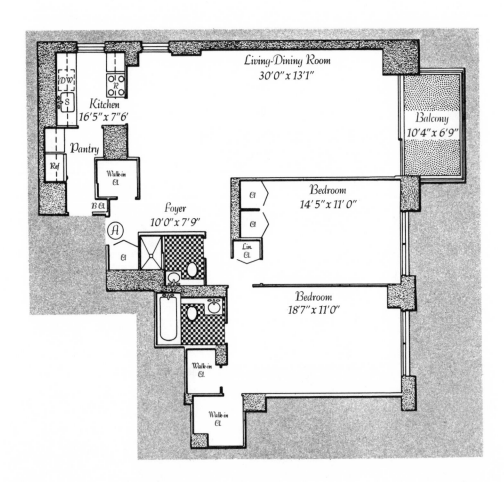

733 Park Avenue

Architect: **Kahn and Jacobs**
Harry F. Green
Builder: **Alexander Muss**
Charles H. Rosenberg
Built: **1971, co-op**

733 Park represents a style of luxuriously exclusive urban living that has all but vanished from the city. It replaces the red brick mansion built in 1904 for Senator Elihu Root, substituting for it a 30-story building containing only 28 apartments. Each typical unit, the least expensive of which carried an initial price of $270,000, consists of 9 rooms and 4½ baths, as shown below. The duplex penthouse, also of 9 rooms, is grandly laid-out as befits its original $526,500 price and $37,635 annual maintenance charge.

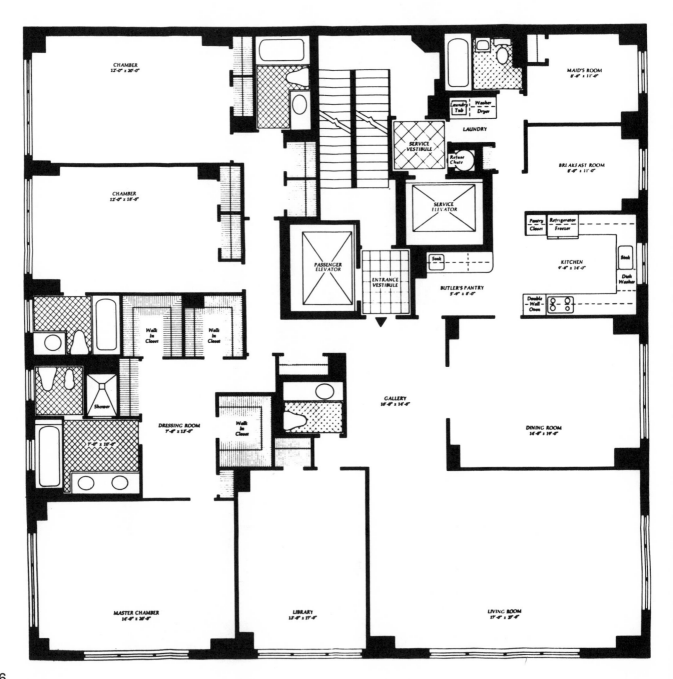

Olympic Tower
641 Fifth Avenue

Architect:	**Skidmore, Owings & Merrill**
Builder:	**Arlen Realty & Development Corporation**
	Victory Development Corporation
Built:	**1974, condominium**

Olympic Tower is an unusual apartment house in two respects. First, it combines in one building, retail stores, a park-like public shopping arcade, commercial office space, and apartments. Second, it provides many of the facilities and services one expects of a hotel, augmented with a number of extra ones. Besides a concierge who can make travel and entertainment arrangements for the residents, there is maid and valet service, a restaurant, a barber shop, a hairdressing salon, and an international newsstand. The building is equipped with a wine cellar, a health club, a stock quotation board, an internal telephone system and an auxiliary emergency power generator, as well as a very sophisticated personal and electronic security system. The two highest floors contain several very large duplexes while the rest of the residential portion of the building consists of eight luxurious but basically conventional apartments to a floor. The plan of a typical corner suite is shown below.

PICTURE CREDITS

INDEX OF ADDRESSES

INDEX OF NAMES